BAD SEX

We Did It, So You Won't Have To

TRUE STORIES
by the writers of Nerve.com

CHRONICLE BOOKS
SAN FRANCISCO

The stories in this collection originally appeared
on Nerve.com, and are used here with permission
of the authors.

Library of Congress Cataloging-in-Publication Data:
Bad sex : we did it, so you won't have to : true stories /
by the writers of Nerve.com.
     p. cm.

ISBN: 978-0-8118-5994-3

1. Sex—Miscellanea. 2. Sex—Anecdotes. 3. Sex—Humor.
I. Nerve.com (Computer file) II. Title.
HQ25.B27 2008
306.702'07—dc22

                                        2007027340

Manufactured in Canada

Designed by Brooke Johnson

10 9 8 7 6 5 4 3 2 1

Chronicle Books LLC
680 Second Street
San Francisco, California 94107

www.chroniclebooks.com

Will Doig

INTRODUCTION

There was a time when we considered all sex a magical, transcendent experience punctuated by a perfect, galaxy-shaking orgasm at the finale. This time was called "virginity."

Then we began to hear about bad sex, and even sampled a bit of it ourselves. We heard people say things like, "Sex is like pizza—even when it's bad, it's still pretty good."

Bad sex is not like pizza. We've had sex that would give you night sweats and cramps if you covered it in pepperoni and mozzarella cheese and took a bite. There was nothing "pretty good" about it.

But we'll take bad sex regardless. And by that, we mean we'll take bad sex over no sex at all. And trust us, we've had some pretty bad sex. Cataclysmic sex. Sex our therapist knows all about.

So why would we prefer the psychic distress, the hurt feelings, the lice, the stalker, the self-doubt, the alibi-shattering hickey, and the cynical worldview that bad sex so often generates? For one thing, bad sex begets good anecdotes. We've absolutely *killed* with our story about the knee-fetish guy with the rolling pin and the motor oil. We like to reveal the scar with a flourish right at the end, like yelling, "The aristocrats!"

But it's not just the comical high jinks we can appreciate. We'll take bad sex over no sex any day, because when it's all said and done, the only thing we learned from no sex was *Law & Order* dialogue. (Lots of it. Verbatim.) From myriad less-than-ideal erotic encounters, however, we've learned plenty, both about ourselves and the awkward, untidy act itself. Sometimes more than we wanted to know. Sometimes more than we could handle. It usually makes for a valuable life lesson wrapped in a pretty good story, a few of which we've gathered for you here.

Like a hostage situation, sometimes you walk away from a bad sexual encounter closer to your partner than you were when you met, bonded for life by a shared traumatic experience. Other times, you simply walk away, wiping the tears and whatever else from your face, sometimes cursing, occasionally limping slightly, but always with a new bit of wisdom.

Porochista Khakpour
THE 20-YEAR-OLD VIRGIN

You Are Different. So Are We. This was the informal motto of
Sarah Lawrence College, where I got a B.A. in nothing (we
didn't have majors), after getting no grades (written evalua-
tions only), based on no tests (just essays). They Pied Pipered
the spectrum of fringe high schoolers with that motto. You
were hazed into their differentness before you ever got there.

My freshman dorm was an English Tudor cottage known
as "The Virgin Dorms." You're supposed to be able to hear the
high-pitched guffaw of generations of spoiled rich girls here. At
SLC, virginity was charming, silly, aesthetically irresistible. It
was '50s cat's-eye glasses, white gloves, and mink stoles. It was
totally adorable—as long as it was totally not real.

This was a school renowned for its impromptu orgies
and sex soirees, where the seventy-thirty ratio of women
to men meant that lesbianism was just another "whatever"

decision. In all my years there, I encountered not a single virgin female. Everybody was nymphomaniacal and/or pansexual and/or "queer."

I, however, was quite heterosexual. This was a problem, since homosexuality and its various incarnations were the law of the land. If you had the audacity—or backward taste—to be a Straight Gal, you were supposed to avoid Straight Guys, since they were obvious agents of the Conservative White Wonder Bread Patriarchy. But they got plenty of action anyway. They were in demand in a black-market sort of way.

Errol seemed pretty standard for a SLC Straight Guy: *Mayflower* ancestry, read only obscure French novels, glass half-to-completely empty, vegan except for sushi, fluent in French and Italian, abstract experimental/early punk/Euro lounge only, turtlenecks, no athletics. I first spotted him as the only other wallflower at the school's annual Coming Out Dance. We made intense eye contact before he was dragged away by a Mohawked blonde. After bumping into each other on the train to Manhattan, I invited him to tea in my Virgin Dorm the next day.

As expected, a few hours into our spiked Earl Greys, our clothes came off and I was offering Errol a dish of condoms as if they were candy. *Not* as expected, he froze. He just stared at the condoms with a mixture of *no comprendo* and *yikes*, like they were exotic currency.

"Surely, dude, you don't think we're, like, not going to use protection?" I finally said, in my best Sarah-Lawrence-ese.

We all had cultivated voices to channel early Audrey Hepburn with a touch of Riot Grrrl.

"No need," he said with rehearsed confidence.

I put the condoms away, and we continued with a long session of all acts that end in the word "job." Afterward, I asked him what the hell had happened.

"Oh, it's just that," he paused as if thinking just how to put it, "you know, I don't do," pausing again, this time with a devilish grin as if he were about to utter something sexy, "It."

Errol was not celibate, not asexual, not gay. He was just not into It. Why? I had to know. He gave me a long lecture about how biological sex was antiprogress, that it was embarrassing to imagine all simpleton earthlings doing It for the sake of It, that it was commercial, pedestrian, perfunctory. "I'll leave it to the one day I really find it imperative to," he said, pausing to wrinkle his nose in deep disgust, "baby-make."

I found myself nodding, mesmerized. Sexual intercourse was for fucking baby-makers! It was 1996 in the avant-garde-lite academy of Sarah Lawrence—of course this reasoning would appeal to any grunge-era-matriculated feminist. This was what "experimenting" in college was all about. No sex was the new sex!

Errol and I formed a cult of sexual pioneers—he the leader, I the lone disciple. Errol became an evangelist of outer-course, constantly scheming new ways and new places to come: hands, mouth, sheets, toys, the odd piece of fruit, basically anything other than vaginal walls. Every session was a triumphant fist-in-the-air moment for the movement.

News of our antiactivities spread. The Straight Girls and Lesbians worshipped Errol for having the ingenuity to keep penetration out of the equation. Straight Guys and Lesbians adored me for being so open-minded and acquiescent, like a magician's lovely assistant who volunteers to get cut up in a coffin over and over.

We kept the campus rumor mill fed with our loud orgasms in the library video rooms, the artillery of sex toys poking out of our bags, our German porn videos tucked under our armpits in place of theory textbooks. Errol and I would sometimes perform demonstrations of preferred foreplay—for instance, eyeball-licking. *Highly erogenous!* Errol would proclaim, breaking it down,

One: Tilt receiver's head and hold.

Two: Breathe on their face. This is sexy.

Three: Have them open eyes wide—no blinking.

Four: Since that's often not possible, force their eyelids open.

Five: Collect saliva around own tongue, not to soak but to lube.

Six: Withdraw tongue in firm form. No Gene Simmons knife-tongue, but not the soggy-nugget dip, either—a solid, resolute tongue ready for some eyeball. *Very* sexy.

Seven: Descend lightly upon middle of eyeball. Go forward lightly, then go back in two strokes.

I'd groan ecstatically, *mmmmm incredible, hon,* before a breathless crowd, and I'd actually feel something like turned on. Well, *charged,* at least, like static-ridden laundry. For a semester, we were the future.

And when the immediate future snuck up on us— summer break—we accepted our separation calmly. *Marathon phone-sextravaganza!* Errol offered optimistically. No contact, no problem!

No problem, except when you leave college and go back to the world of normal people—people with jobs and bills and debt who live in suburban wastelands, drive bad American cars, and are related to you—you are forced to come to terms with who you are. You Are Not Different. It's ugly. You remind yourself no rich daddy paid your way there: you're the sole Virgin Dormee on scholarship. Your parents actually eat meat and potatoes—no macrobiotic options at this cafeteria. They've never heard of croquet or Kierkegaard. All the differences come crashing down, and there you are: ponytailed, in jean shorts and Adidas, eating fries with your primary-school best friend in the local McDonald's parking lot, realizing that no, sexual intercourse is *just what your people do.*

But summer was not forever. Sophomore year began, and I was back in old form—deconstructed dress shirts, gartered fishnets, metallic lipstick—and picking at cafeteria sashimi with golden chopsticks while chain-smoking Nat Sherman Fantasias. Errol greeted me by making a cluster of artistically arranged hickeys on my neck. He had made some exciting purchases, he wanted me to know: a shiny anal vibrator, not to mention hermaphrodite porn from Prague. It was all back to abnormal!

But the thing was, I felt suddenly rusty about our old ways. The rationale was foggier than before. Our audience was gone. There was a whole new flock of Virgin Dormees for the campus to corrupt. What use were we now?

Still, it never occurred to me to doubt Errol until a mutual friend approached me and asked me last year's question: why I thought Errol would do everything but It anyway.

I was still a cult member. I beamed dumbly like a TomKat-era Katie Holmes, far too indoctrinated in my partner's ways for self-consciousness or shame. "That vaginal-intercourse shit is so our parents' generation, so old school, so mainstream, you know?"

Mutual Friend groaned, having heard our shtick too much by now. "I think you should know that your man is not some genius sex artist. He's a *virgin*."

I laughed. Oh, how I laughed! Too loud, too long, for what felt like hours, days even, weeks, that laughter of delirious, deluded women. The idea drove me nuts. It was so painfully obvious, and yet I had never examined the fine print beneath Errol's preferences. Virginity was one thing when tagged stylishly to a girl's dorm room, but to a guy—the horror! Adult males were just not virgins!

I had to deprogram myself, make a definitive break from Errol. But how? The answer was standing in front of me: cheat on him. With Mutual Friend, who was incredibly average by real-world standards and therefore exotic at SLC.

Once in MF's room, I took the reins and arranged him on top of me. We proceeded to engage in very biologically programmed, traditional sexual intercourse. Like any first sexual encounter, it was slightly off—too fast, too soft, too dry, too quiet, then too loud—but the awkwardness was a beautiful thing to me. In all my time with Errol, I had forgotten that I loved Intercourse the Ritual.

Soon, I became that secretly coveted thing, The Girlfriend. We did it once a day. I got infections. I considered oral contraceptives. Upon the first condom rupture, I skipped to the nurse's office and expressed pregnancy panic like I was collecting a Girl Scout badge. When I downed the morning-after pill with a swig of beer, it was like being home again. I was with a man who did It and had done It before, an It never exceeding anything more than pure, simple, the-way-your-grandparents-did-It, mediocre Intercoursing!

Meanwhile, Errol disappeared. Onward to some new disciple, I'm sure. I always thought of him as my virgin, but I suppose I could never prove it. In an anthropology class that year, I learned that only in the KwaZulu-Natal Midlands of South Africa can tribal leaders determine male virginity through a simple physical exam. Not only can they detect a "male hymen," they can tell by how you pee (projectile stream = virgin; messy spray = done It) and by the shade of your knees versus your legs.

In Errol's case, it's a shame eyeballs don't tell tales.

Sarah Thyre
NIGHT OF THE LIVING EX-GIRLFRIEND

During my junior year at Louisiana State University, I vacillated between majoring in English, so I could be a fever-dreaming, impoverished poet, and microbiology, so I could be a focused, serious doctor, like the ones on TV.

"That's all well and good," I would say to my egotistical blowhard colleagues. *"But there's a life at stake here!"*

Spring semester found me back on the premed track. Dr. Rheinhardt taught the only section of pathology, a required course. Everyone spoke of him in frightened tones. He scheduled class for the prime collegiate hangover hour of 7:30 A.M.

I'd sit there with a $1.99 Student Union early-bird breakfast special in my belly: two eggs over easy, grits, toast, and a large Diet Coke, sliding around on top of last night's gallon of nickel beer. I was transported by Dr. Rheinhardt's monologues on death and disease. The only thing he paused to do was ridicule the Bow Heads, sorority girls who sat in an overachieving line across the front row. Scarlett Kerrit was the head Bow Head, with the crispest, perkiest grosgrain bow perched above her claw bangs.

"Dr. Rheinhardt, Dr. Rheinhardt!" cawed Scarlett one morning, flapping her returned pop quiz in the air. "I don't understand why you deducted points on question three."

Dr. Rheinhardt turned around from the blackboard and removed the unlit pipe from his mouth, methodically, lovingly, lying it on the podium.

"Because, my dear," he said, "I *can*."

"Dr. R., don't be that way," Scarlett sugar-talked. "I believe I have a valid complaint."

Dr. Rheinhardt put his pipe back between his lips and gave it a wet, smokeless suck.

"Complaints," he said, "are never valid."

Scarlett's mouth opened and closed and opened and closed like a moray eel's.

I felt a frisson of glee. That's when I noticed Cool Guy noticing me.

I had noticed him the first day of class. I don't know why I called him Cool Guy.

Not My Type, Part One: he had a beard.

Not My Type, Part Two: he reeked of Drakkar Noir.

Not My Type, Parts Three to Twelve: he always sat with the Bow Heads.

"Fraternity dropout!" I'd heard Scarlett Kerrit screech at him, many times.

That he was ever in a fraternity implied passable skills in the art of date-rapery; that he dropped out and had a beard made me think he had tempered those skills with an atypically sensitive, nonconformist approach.

"No darling, *you* tell *me* how forcefully you would like to be entered against your will," I imagined him saying, then immediately tried to unimagine it.

Cool Guy smiled at me, like he was reading my mind.

Totally My Type, Parts One through Infinity: he carried himself with the same intellectual hauteur as my abusive ex-boyfriend, Stephen. They had both gone to the Catholic boys' school in New Orleans renowned for turning out bright, Latin-spouting young men with acute Madonna/Whore complexes.

Within a month, Dr. Rheinhardt had bullied and battered almost half the students into dropping his class. Those of us brave enough to stay were condensed into new groups to perform our lab experiments. Cool Guy and I ended up in the same group with another guy named Chip.

Chip was what you'd call a nontraditional student. Forty-two years old, he'd flunked his way through every Catholic school in southeast Louisiana and had been doing time at a series of community colleges ever since.

"You look familiar to me," Chip said.

We retraced the steps of our lives, figuring out that ten years ago, he used to go out with my next-door neighbor's daughter.

"I must've seen you one night," I said, "when you came to pick Sandy up for a date."

"We didn't really date. Mostly we just sat out in her drive-way in my Firebird doing blow," Chip said. "Which reminds me, I can get government-grade Ecstasy if you ever need some. Two dollars a hit."

I took one look at Chip's rotted lower front teeth and wrote down his phone number.

For our first experiment, we had to collect blood from a rabbit.

"'Scuse me, 'scuse me," I bellowed, elbowing my way up to the rabbit with a syringe of ketamine, an animal tranquil-izer. Right away, I wanted to make it clear to Chip and Cool Guy that I was no shrinking violet. The rabbit scrambled as I shot the ketamine into its haunch. In two seconds it was lying there panting, its irises rolled up into its skull.

"Special kayyyyyyy," Chip said, giving a low whistle. "Looks pretty good to me."

The Iranian grad student supervising us gave Chip a sharp look through the eyehole in her veil. She quickly pock-eted the vial of ketamine.

"Silence!" she said. "The time for the bleeding has come."

To prep the area, I used a Bic razor to shave the fur off the rabbit's ear.

"Nice shave, how much you charge?" Cool Guy said, coming up with a twenty-five-gauge needle, its diameter nearly the same as a drinking straw's. His arm brushed against my chest as he reached out to put a hand on the rabbit's leg. "Take it easy, Cottontail."

My hands were trembling. The rabbit's skin became transparent, and I could see the pulsing network of veins and arteries inside its body, pumping and bulging with sweet, hot liquid.

Cool Guy stuck the needle into the rabbit's ear vein the way a lady slips her outstretched leg into a stocking, decanting enough blood to fill two shot glasses.

My ears began to ring and my upper lip felt clammy. I clung to the edge of the gurney, willing myself not to pass out. I'm pretty macho that way.

We added some chemicals to the blood. It would take a couple hours to read the results. Chip, Cool Guy, and I decided to pass the time over at the Library, a bar next to campus. Their slogan was, *When your mama asks where you been, tell her you was at the Library!*

Within an hour we had drunk five pitchers of Abita Turbodog ale.

"So, it just makes you wonder," Chip said, concluding a long, rambling gripe about his job at the vet school's crematorium. "Am I like, the Hitler of cats?"

Cool Guy and I were too busy making out on the banquette to answer. Out of politeness, I opened one eye. Chip sat across from us, his beer-glazed expression melancholy in the light from a neon sign.

"It's gettin' late," he sighed, after watching us for ten more minutes. "Y'all mind finishing up back at the lab? I gotta go give my mom her interferon shot."

Upon our bleary return to the lab, Cool Guy and I stumbled smack into Scarlett Kerrit. A hardy Bow Head, she had weathered Dr. Rheinhardt's withering put-downs and stayed in the class.

"Y'all smell lahk a beer gahden!" she said to Cool Guy, slapping his arm.

"What?" Cool Guy said.

"It'sh a very old-fashioned shaying," I said, pulling test tubes of spun blood out of the centrifuge.

"I can't believe y'all!" Scarlett went on, still addressing only Cool Guy. "Y'all're all . . . *drawnk!*"

"Duh," Cool Guy said, putting a rack of dirty beakers in the autoclave. He grabbed me, bent me over the lab bench, and licked the full stretch of my throat.

Eat shit, Scarlett!

Cool Guy and I left the lab, heading straight to his place, a cute little one-bedroom cottage. Its dominant decorative feature was a twenty-foot albino python coiled inside a cage the size of a British telephone booth. He put on the twelve-inch extended version of Bob Marley's "Exodus."

"Fire this up for me, will ya?" Cool Guy said, packing marijuana into one end of an elaborate network of glass tubing and Pyrex vessels.

"So this is where all our lab equipment went," I said, trying to focus my eyes in the room's only light source, a flashing traffic signal.

"I carved this part myself out of an old toy boat from my childhood," Cool Guy said, wrapping his lips around a wooden mouthpiece five feet away.

As I lit the pot, he sucked the smoke through the series of tubes and flasks.

"Thanks, babe," he grinned, reclining into a mattress leaning against the wall, the only furniture in the room.

"Why do you hang out with Scarlett and them?" I asked.

"I don't hang out with them. I just sat there on the first day of class so I kept sitting there," Cool Guy said. "See that field out back? Ag-school pasture. Tomorrow morning we can go pick psilocybin mushrooms right off the cow patties. Trip our balls off all weekend long."

"I'll save you some money on pot because I don't smoke," I said, my voice sounding like a schoolmarm's.

"What?!" Cool Guy said.

"It doesn't get me high," I said. "So I don't bother."

In truth, it rendered me less articulate than I liked to fancy myself.

"Trust me, this'll get you high," Cool Guy assured me, leading me over to the wooden mouthpiece.

The next thing I knew it was morning, or almost. Somewhere, a foreign-sounding doorbell was ringing.

I sat upright. I was in a strange bed, between unfamiliar, hunter-green sheets. The doorbell rang. And rang. And rang.

The doorbell sounded foreign because it was the opening notes of "La Cucaracha."

In the dawn's early light I could make out Cool Guy next to me, snoring heavily. Oh, right. Him. I looked closer. His beard had crumbs in it.

After a few minutes, the doorbell stopped ringing. An insistent rapping began on the small window above our heads. The rapping stopped, and seconds later, the doorbell started up again. Then, more rappity-tap-tap-TAP-RAP-RAP-RAP-SLAP-bedippy-DAP on the window.

Finally, Cool Guy stirred.

"Shit," he mumbled, rolling over.

"What's going on?" I whispered.

"Probably just my old girlfriend," he said.

He seemed content to ignore what now sounded like pounding on every window and door of the apartment. A hysterical voice seeped in through the walls.

"Matt! Matty! Matthew!" it mewled.

"Who's Matty?" I whispered.

Cool Guy looked at me, disgusted.

"That's not funny," he said.

You're telling me, I thought.

"Let me in, Matty," whined the voice. "I know you're in there!"

The banging, now back at the front door, crescendoed in a shattering crash.

"Fuck!" Cool Guy yelled, leaping out of bed.

Something told me it was best to stay put.

"What are you, crazy?" his voice came from the living room. "You broke the fuckin' window!"

"Is she in there? Lemme see 'er!"

"No! Gina—don't!"

"I'maw fight her!"

Thumping and dragging noises came from the living room. I looked around for a weapon. That four-foot bong in the corner would do nicely.

"I just wanna talk to her, Matthew."

"No—stop it, Gina! I broke up with you, remember?"

The bile of superiority rose thick in my throat.

"Matthew, you love me," Gina sobbed. "I love you, Matty. I know what you need. Matt. I love you."

Matty and Gina. Gina 'n' Matt. Togethuh Forevah. The sobs died down to whimpers, then rustling, like they were fighting over a bag of potato chips. My stomach growled. I wondered what the albino python thought of all this.

"Enough," Cool Guy said, sounding tired. "Gina, stop."

"No, honey. I'm gonna show you how much I love you."

"Don't do this, Gina," he said. "Put your shirt back on."

"Kiss me, Matty. Please. Just kiss me."

Yes, they were definitely sick and deserved only each other. Still, I jealously strained to hear any slurping noises. I mean, *he better not be all kissing her and shit.*

I couldn't hear anything. Drowning out all noise from the living room was a catchy, fingerpickin' lick that began playing in my head.

Dare-dare-dare-delare
dare-dare-dare-dare-dare

It was the guitar intro to the Allman Brothers' song "One Way Out," the song about being trapped upstairs in some chick's bedroom when her man comes in the door downstairs.

Ain't but one way out baby, and Lord I just can't go out the door.

My life was now officially a ten on the Southern-Fried-Boogie-Rock Scale.

In the song, there's only one way out: the window. Not such a bad idea. I kneeled on the bed and moved the towel that hung like a curtain over the window.

Alas, I couldn't escape through the window like Gregg Allman. The pane didn't actually open. Furthermore, I could now see this was no cute cottage—it was one of those fake houses that was really a TRAILER!

I ripped the towel down off its staples and wrapped it around my fist, intending to punch out the glass.

I froze, picturing myself standing outside in the Ag-school pasture, surrounded by cowshit sundaes topped with cherry-colored psychedelic mushrooms. Naked.

Where wuz my clothes at?

Had I actually thought that, in that accent? This whole situation reeked like a stained rag hanging out of the gas tank of a rusty old Chevy truck, and nobody stunk worse than me. *I.*

"Dammit, Gina!" Cool Guy roared.

The music in my head stopped like someone had yanked the needle off a record.

"You know I never liked your striptease act," Cool Guy continued. His mouth sounded full. "I *hate* you, Gina. Get *out*. Now. *Leave.*"

A trail of sniffled, impotent threats ended with the soft slam of the front door.

Cool Guy came back into the bedroom. I pretended to be asleep. He got back in bed, still nude, and spooned up against me. His beard grazed my neck, sending a chill down my spine. He started rubbing in that insistent way that heterosexual women all over the world have known at some point or another. He rubbed and rubbed, sawing away at my butt cheeks. I pushed out my behind in a fake-sleepy "knock it off" gesture, which he completely misread.

"Ohhhhhhhh," he said, his voice quavering like an old gold prospector's. "Ya wan' me t'stick it in yer asshole, babe?"

If someone's body could fill up with vomit, it would have been mine, at that moment. I clenched my butt cheeks together and let out an embarrassingly fake snore.

Fooled, Cool Guy rolled onto his back and took care of himself.

Rocked to sleep by the motion, I dozed off for real. It was a pleasant, unexamined sleep.

"Babe. Babe, wake up," Cool Guy said, rattling my shoulder. "I made you some breakfast."

Opening my eyes, I was nearly blinded by the ugliest blouse I had ever seen. It was gray with a wacky, cubist design sprinkled across it, a hideous pattern some horribly misguided person had deemed casual yet manly.

The buttons were shaped like scarab beetles.

There was also a do-rag.

"I call it marijuana marmalade," said the lips in the middle of the beard atop the blouse below the turquoise bandanna. "I made it myself, with a gelling agent I stole from pathology lab."

There was no way out.

I took a bite. It tasted like a moldy shower curtain.

"Mmmmmm," I gagged, licking my fingers. "Dude. Nice blouse."

Steve Almond
CHESTFRO AGONISTES

Why, exactly, did I believe it would be "sexy" and "hot" to have my girlfriend wax my chest? I can offer no good answer to this question today, ten years after the event. I could offer no good answer at the time. What I could offer was a rather far-fetched fantasy, which involved (as far-fetched fantasies so often do) a Byzantine set of subfantasies. They ran something like this:

1. My girlfriend and I would do a whole bunch of Ecstasy;

2. At a certain point, she would disappear into her closet and emerge dressed like Catwoman;

3. Warm wax would magically appear in her paw;

4. She would caress said wax onto my chest, while purring nasty things into my ear;

5. She would pull my hair and tell me what a dirty little monkey I was;

6. The wax would harden, seductively;

7. I would make monkey noises and rub my raging man-bat against her;

8. She would slap me and my boner, but not so hard as to make me weep;

9. She would start to pull the wax off, viciously, with great, grinning flourishes;

10. This would sting, but in an awesome, S&M kind of way;

11. My smooth, naked chest would look so manly that she would be compelled to lick the entire surface area;

12. Some very serious fucking would ensue.

I don't suppose I have to tell you that my expectations were a bit on the high side. What still astounds me is how spectacularly wrong it all went. And this wasn't your standard sexual miscalculation. The old whipped-cream-up-the-cooter-begets-monster-yeast-infection. The I'm-feeling-crazy-tonight-are-you-feeling-crazy-baby-back-sprain-mambo. The let's-do-it-in-a-public-place-oh-hi-officer-deluxe. To which I say (and have said): Ho ho ho. No harm, no foul. Kids.

This was something darker, more malignant. At the risk of getting myself banned for life from the Church of American Sanctimony, I would characterize the episode as the Guanta-namo Bay of sexual relations.

A few relevant notes to begin:

The wax. It was not the inviting substance I'd envisioned. It was, instead, a thick, pungent glop the color of earwax. I don't know where my girlfriend purchased the stuff. But she heated it on her stove (in a recycled soup can!) to the approximate temperature of lava.

My chest. And specifically the number of hairs upon it. I have not done an exact audit, but I am going to approximate a googol. I am talking about a mat on the order of Austin Powers. To give you the proper mental image, I should note that a friend of mine once referred to this region, not unkindly, as my chestfro.

My girlfriend. She was sweet. She was gorgeous. She was, rather sweetly, rather gorgeously, a sadist. She also happened to be Cuban American, which lent her an unresolved, self-dramatizing quality. There was a pronounced violent streak in her family. She worked out a great deal. Although she stood less than five feet tall and weighed a hundred pounds in sports bra and garters, I feel safe in observing that she could have beaten me to a pulp.

Me. I was frightfully insecure, with good cause, as I was living in South Miami Beach, where everyone was 3.5 times more attractive than me. My girlfriend had made considerable efforts to remedy my chronic gawkiness: a new haircut, new glasses, new clothes. The chest waxing was, in part, one of these self-improvement projects.

And this is where the problem began, I believe. Beneath the chest-waxing-as-hot-sexual-come-on lay a more problematic paradigm: the chest-waxing-as-elimination-of-excessive-Jew-hair. Be that as it may, we went forward with the plan. She spread newspapers on the floor of her living room and put the wax on to boil and I stripped to my skivvies and practiced monkey noises.

The problems began upon application. My girlfriend removed the can of wax from the stove with a pair of tongs. I lay on my back, giggling nervously. She dipped a tongue depressor and ran it along my clavicle. I felt I was perhaps burning. She moved down to the pectoral region. I tried to be stoic about this, while also suggesting (in a hoarse whisper) that we should maybe let the wax cool down.

My girlfriend scoffed. The wax had to be hot. She regularly waxed her own legs. And, as she had informed me regally, she had her "twat" waxed—presumably for my benefit—on numerous occasions, so anything I might have to say about pain held no sway with her. Indeed, the process was already appealing to her sadism in profound and unwholesome ways.

Let me pause here to point out a physiological fact: chest skin is really sensitive. I'm not going to put it up against twat skin (or whatever I should be calling it), but I will say that the chest, in terms of nerve endings, makes back skin seem like a hide. Even more delicate is the skin of the stomach, and specifically the strip that extends from belly button to pelvic bone (a.k.a. "The Highway to Hell"), which, in the interest of consistency, my girlfriend decided needed to be waxed, too.

About the wax, upon drying: I had envisioned neat little strips ready for the plucking. The reality was more like a small, turbulent sea of gunk. It felt like I had a great deal of gum stuck to my chest. I smelled like a giant crayon.

But the real trouble started with the removal phase. I was prepared for a brisk, temporary pain, of the sort one encounters when yanking off a Band-Aid. This was more like stabbing at road rash. Alas, my girlfriend, for all her experience in the leg department, was totally overmatched by my lush chestal thicket. For every square inch of wax, there were somewhere in the area of 19,000 hairs to be yanked. That is—to put it in technical terms—a fuckuva lot of adhesive force. Add to this the fact that the wax was slippery. My girlfriend couldn't get a good grip. She eventually hacked the wax up into slices. This did no good. (There was also the problem of my conduct; I writhed a fair amount.)

The result was a bunch of half-assed yanking, which loosened the hairs in such a manner that I suffered profound epidermal trauma while not actually freeing any of the hairs from their roots. I cannot remember precisely what was said during the ensuing twenty minutes. Here is an approximation, with the yelps edited out.

Me: Ow! Please. Please, don't—fuck.

Her: It's almost out.

Me: You have to do it faster, really—no! Ow! Fuck! Please move to another strip, that part really—owwww!

Her: Stop being such a baby.

Me: Please, sweetie. Please, I'm not joking.

Her: Lie still. Just fucking lie still and let me.

Me: Owww. You fucking bitch. You fucking mean bitch.

We were not communicating effectively.

We didn't even make it to the nipples, though certainly my girlfriend had designs. What actually brought this sad ballet to a close was the initial (and final) moment of success: my girlfriend managed to tear free a single, mangled chunk of wax-and-hair. I climbed to my feet and marched to the bathroom and looked in the mirror and saw dabs of blood on my tortured skin.

It occurred to me at this point that we were probably not going to have sex.

I returned to the living room, encased in my hacked-up exoskeleton, and informed my girlfriend that I'd had enough. She looked at me with an expression that traveled beyond contempt, into the deeper regions of pity. "Fine," she said, and went to get Chinese takeout.

It was unclear what I should do. I was furious and humiliated. She was disgusted. We were in a fight. I considered placing a call for help, but to whom? Was there a local support group for the sadomasochistically challenged?

In the end, I found an old pair of scissors and cut away most of the wax, then shaved my chest and belly with my girlfriend's razor. And I must admit that I felt, for a few hours there, really young and hot. And gay.

Then the itching began.

I spent the next month clawing at my chest. My girlfriend and I soon broke up. But I learned a valuable lesson. Namely, that most healthy relationships should not depend on the administration of hot wax for sexual enhancement. And, of course, that the enemy of my chest hair is the enemy of me.

Rachel Shukert

EUROPE, HO!

As I crouched half-naked in the upstairs staff toilet of a suburban Paris hotel, even the impressively heady mixture of France, kir, and daunting expectations of the eighteen other North American teenage girls on my trip could not quite persuade me to lose my virginity to the guy who manned the steam table at the dinner buffet. In retrospect, this was probably an excellent decision. At the time, however, as I rubbed the bulge in his polyester work pants with the heel of my hand, I felt my failure keenly.

"*Oui, oui, oui,*" he murmured, with clear sarcasm.

Next time I was in Europe, I vowed to do better.

The next time was several years later. Those years that brought with them the added previous participation in actual sexual intercourse. Past that initial hurdle, I figured sleeping with a non-American would be easy. After all, non-America was crawling with them.

But two days into my second European holiday, an unfortunate bicycle accident in Amsterdam left me with a broken nose, two black eyes, and a missing tooth. Nobody, not even a matter-of-fact Dutchman, was going to fuck me. Even if the bridge of my nose didn't ooze gritty pus every time I nodded my head, my mouth was far too swollen and bloody to offer much pleasure to any but the most dogged of sadists.

My fantasies of lovers from many lands were quickly shaping up to be just that—fantasies. I began to consign myself to the idea that I would become one of *those* women, the kind who melt at the barest hint of an accent on a man carrying a purse, who complains bitterly of her lumpen husband's refusal to eat any food ending with a vowel. But after countless couplings with natives of Cincinnati, Nyack, and San Antonio; of Tulsa, Portland, and San Antonio; of Duluth, Pittsburgh, and San Antonio; the opportunity for foreign fulfillment knocked once again.

I met him in Vienna, at the opening-night party of a show I was touring with. Bound by an immediate physical attraction but hindered by a lack of meaningful common language, we were soon locked into a guileless impasse of grinning and nodding, obscure, befuddled dignitaries eagerly struggling to make a good impression on the powerful.

"You are finding Vienna . . . " he said, trailing off uncertainly. His coaxing eyes were bright and laced on all sides by deep lines. He was at least fifteen years older than me (twenty, I learned later), which, frankly, added to my excitement.

"Oh, yes. I found it just fine. Well, the pilot helped," I joked reflexively.

He stared at me curiously. I downed my glass of wine in one gulp, hoping to asphyxiate myself.

"It's so beautiful here," I added.

"You are from New York City?"

"Well, not originally. I grew up in Omaha. Nebraska."

"Nebraska? What is it?" This is, I am afraid to say, not an unfamiliar question.

"It's a state. Right in the middle of the U.S.," I said cheerfully, without a trace of the annoyance I display for the East Coasters who think I am from Oklahoma.

"Nebraska. Yes." He smiled. "Good."

Three bottles of wine later, we were pressed against each other in a cobblestone alley, kissing feverishly. His breath was acrid with cigarettes and liquor, and he forced my jaw open to accept his tongue, which lay heavy and thick in my mouth. Usually, this kind of aggressive tooth-kissing is a deal breaker for me, as it puts me in mind of the wee fistlike monsters that gnaw their way through John Hurt's stomach in *Alien,* but I told myself, *I'm open to new things. Isn't that what travel is all about?*

"Come, please, now to my home," he whispered throatily, kneading my neck hard with his chin.

I declined. I had to get up early. I was jet-lagged. I was too drunk. I would get lost on the way back. All valid, all nonsense.

Visibly disappointed, he silently walked me back to my hotel. I found myself resenting him more and more with each step. *What the hell is his problem?* I sulked. *It's not like I'm obligated to go home with someone I just met. An American guy would know that. An American guy would just call me later or something.* And then, a sobering prospect—*Could it be that I'm only comfortable around Americans?*

On the steps outside the lobby, he kissed me softly, and left, pressing a small object into my hand. I uncurled my fingers. Nestled in the palm of my hand was a little ball of shiny blue rubber, the kind you can drop out of a window and find, still bouncing, on the sidewalk days later.

At four A.M., sleepless with jet lag and self-loathing, I headed across the street in my pajamas to one of the twenty-four-hour snack kiosks that pepper the streets of Vienna and ordered a *Käsekrainer*, a sausage served in a long bun. Tentatively, I bit down. A stream of runny white cheese spurted out and hit me directly in the face.

This was clearly a sign.

The next afternoon, the dour concierge presented me with a card left in my message box. On one side was a tiny, perfect map of Nebraska, rendered painstakingly by hand. On the other, a phone number.

That night, after a meal of Wiener schnitzel (Wiener schnitzel!) we sat in front of the large picture window in his airy loft, gazing out at the illuminated city. He touched my face gently and murmured something in German.

"What?" I asked.

"I say, 'You are a beautiful child.'"

In a single phrase, all my personal vanity, father issues, and compulsive needs to be coddled and infantilized were addressed and dispatched with the calm efficiency of a Swiss watchmaker. If ten thousand chimpanzees, implanted with the cloned brains of Casanova and Sigmund Freud, were gathered in a vast laboratory, chained to typewriters, with the voice of God reading aloud my complete psychiatric records and unflattering testimonials from everyone I've ever dated (documents that, I am sure, share a disheartening similarity), in seventy years or more they could never discover a line that would get my clothes off faster.

He put some Strauss on the stereo and we waltzed naked as he explained the importance of three-quarter time in the Viennese sensibility. I smiled adoringly. He brought out a bottle of sweet white wine, made from tiny grapes found wild in the snowy peaks of the Alps, then poured it over my body and licked it from my breasts. I smiled adoringly. I was being extravagantly seduced by an oh-so-worldly European old enough to be my father; I had quantum-leaped into that *Saturday Night Live* sketch with Christopher Walken. His accented dialogue expounded on the techniques of erotic massage and the properties of true French Champagne, and for the first time in my life, I had not even the faintest impulse toward sarcasm. He carried me into the bedroom and proceeded to tongue my pubic hair with aplomb. I lay still, chilled Riesling trickling uncomfortably into my belly button.

The evening suffered a slight hiccup when I deduced that the rubbery, tirelike band gathered around the base of his penis was not just a physiological quirk but a *foreskin*. I became so flustered that I was forced to bring the blowjob portion of the evening to an abrupt halt. (My basic sexual training was conducted in the summer camps and conclaves of affluent American Jewry, and little since has challenged its essential thesis.) The rest went smoothly, as I'd hoped.

The next morning, I woke up alone. He had left early for work. Dreamily, I was toying with one of the empty condom packets on the nightstand, perched atop *The Collected Works of Joseph Beuys,* when panic struck. I didn't recognize this brand of condom. Every single fucking word on it was in *German,* for Christ's sake—a language that had hardly proven trustworthy in the past—and nowhere could I find the comforting word "latex" on the wrapper. Shouldn't the word for "latex" be the same in every language? Could these be, horror of horrors, *lambskin* condoms? The condoms that, according to my seventh grade *Human Growth & Development* textbook, were porous enough to allow all manner of vermin and infectious agents through? "Oh, God," I said aloud, my heart in my stomach. "Oh, God. Oh, God. Oh, God."

Immediately, I felt ashamed. Why did my scurrilous mind have to ruin what had been a perfectly romantic night, a night full of passion and mystery? Movies are made about such a night, movies where middle-aged women whose husbands have left them for game-show hostesses are egged on by girlfriends with suspiciously lesbian haircuts into redemption through fucking foreign men.

But we were in his country. I was the foreigner.

He called late that afternoon. "I am very touched," he said. "All the girls I have made sex with, you are the only who makes the bed. This is an American thing?"

"No," I said. "It's something I picked up in the army."

We made plans for a late dinner.

BODILY FLUIDS

Ben Brown

THE LAST HURRAH

I'm midway through what I'm sure is going to be—*has* to be—one of my best sexual performances of all time. Head down at my girlfriend's right shoulder, I've just settled in for the long haul: rhythm strong, breathing regular. Then she stops me and says, "Be careful of my smallpox."

This is a fringe benefit of having sex with a member of the U.S. Army. I raise my head from my girlfriend's collarbone, careful not to muss the arm of her brown, standard-issue T-shirt. It's the only thing protecting me from the vaccine: millions of smallpox-virus cells festering on her arm in preparation for Saddam's purportedly imminent onslaught. I try not to think about a painful, sticky death. She adjusts her sleeve and gives me a wink, and we get back to business. Careful business.

On her left arm, she's got a hard lump under the skin. "Feel it," she had said to me over dinner. "That's typhoid." She's had all the vaccines you can get, not including botulism, which apparently isn't worth worrying about.

The army tells soldiers not to have any intimate contact with their friends and family after being dosed with smallpox. "No hugging. Do not play with small children. And try not to have sex." There's a bit of concern in the officer community—of which my girlfriend is a part—that they're going to inadvertently cause a smallpox outbreak that will terrorize America. This is the scenario: A dozen highly contagious officers board commercial airliners destined for points abroad. Shoulders are rubbed. Virus is transmitted.

I'm putting myself at risk. This is sort of a one-last-hurrah thing we're doing. In less than twenty-four hours, she has to board a commercial airliner and fly to Chicago, England, Kuwait.

She's only going for a two-week training mission, but with Bush and Powell shooting off at the mouth about imminent threats and orange alerts, we both figure that now is the best time to say goodbye the way adults say goodbye. When she called, I packed a duffel of supplies, told my roommate not to wait up, and deployed myself to her army base.

The way I see it, sex with her is my patriotic duty. I can't send her off to war without one last orgasm. And I have to do a good job. There can be no premature ejaculation, no broken condom. In her bedroom, I have the anxiety of a virgin. Should I perform oral sex? Should I go slow? Fast? Hard? Does it ruin everything if I ask if she came? What does a soldier need to prepare for six months of combat? What about a year in the desert? I think about the fact that she could die. This could be the last fuck of her life.

I am totally unprepared for the pressure.

Next to the bed, there's a stack of decontaminating bandages. While my girlfriend's in the bathroom putting her pants back on, I pick one up and scan the instructions. *Should your bandage fall off while you sleep*, it reads, *immediately remove all of your bedclothes and wash them SEPARATELY from your normal laundry. Then, thoroughly wash yourself with antibacterial soap, being careful not to scrape the exposed area.* It's a good thing they didn't dose her on the butt; I'd have exposed myself a dozen times already. After she returns to bed and we're lying next to each other (hands at our sides, of course, to avoid any potentially disastrous spooning), my girlfriend asks if I can recognize the symptoms of smallpox. Headache. Fever. Loss of appetite. Nodules all over your skin.

"You're kidding," I say. "Right? I haven't been exposed. Right?"

"It pays to be paranoid," she says. "I'll give you the number of an army doctor, just in case you start showing signs of an outbreak."

We fall asleep, managing to assume a position in which I'm neither exposing myself to smallpox nor chafing her sore, typhoid arm. During the night, I wake up in three distinct panics. Each time, I check to make sure I haven't dislodged her bandage. Around four A.M., my arm starts itching, and I'm convinced it's the pox. I consider waking her up, but figure I probably won't die before the morning.

And I don't. When I take my girlfriend and her four duffel bags of gear to the airport, three national guardsmen recognize her as an officer. They rush over and take her bags to the ticket counter. This is a good thing, because even one is too heavy for me to lift. She and I have an awkward moment, standing there in the high security drop-off lane. It wouldn't be good for her, careerwise, if the other soldiers saw her kissing me, a punk with blue hair and piercings. So we hug, and she promises to write me a letter as soon as she's settled into wherever she's going. I promise to send her a mix CD. Then she leaves with the guardsmen to board her plane.

The next day, I've got a headache, a sore throat, and I don't feel like getting out of bed. My roommate pops his head in and says, "Oh shit! You've got the 'thrax!"

But I don't. I just miss her.

Monica Drake
THE SPLATTER ARTIST

So I met this guy at school, or maybe it was at a punk rock
show, some kind of music, I don't remember but I know I'd
seen him around long before we ever talked and the thing
was, he was great. He had light brown skin and an easy smile,
strong arms, and paint on his clothes. He painted on big can-
vases in a warehouse in an illegal squatters' space downtown.
He looked in my eyes when he talked. He was hard in all the
right ways but I guessed he'd be secretly adoring, maybe up
for adventure.

We drank cheap beer together because that's what spoke
to the Bohemian in us. Why go for froufrou and fancy drinks?
We were not of the bourgeoisie, not yet, not then. I lived in a
studio apartment. He—let's call him Kerouac, for the hell of
it, and of course that wasn't his name, but it would've been
nice had it been—might not have lived anywhere. Maybe he
slept in his painter's squat. Maybe he walked the streets.

Let's call him Basquiat, or Pollock, or Henry Miller. Why not? You get my point: old-school romanticism, the wild-man artist. It was all over him. I was all over him. Kurt Cobain? No, it wasn't like that. He wasn't so troubled, at least not in any obvious way.

One day in my studio, we were drinking beer and stacking the bottles into pyramids. We were drawing together, in the light of my big open windows. Other people came and went, dropping in to share their stash, their company, their aimless ways. I had a pack of oil pastels. Basquiat and I, Kerouac and I, we had almost as much paper as we had time on our hands. We drew and we drank, and before the sun even moved below the midafternoon roofline of the city outside the windows, we were smashed.

He leaned over and used the side of an oil pastel to run a long, broad line of red down the thigh of my worn jeans. I felt the heat of his hand as it followed that line, from my crotch to my knee, over the curve of muscles and bones.

What could I do?

I wrapped an arm over his shoulders, pulled him close. I drew a blue smiley on his shirt. Basquiat's shirt was thin and slid over his skin, his body, his pecs.

Oil pastel is smeary and thick. It stays put and travels, both. The day was warm, the apartment sweltering, and the pastels were soft under our hands. He, this man of mine, drew long eyelashes down my cheek, made the pastel into makeup, but it wasn't good makeup, wasn't willing, it was erratic. I drew on his face, too, and when he pulled off his shirt I drew on his shoulder, down over his hairless brown chest. The pastel crayon tugged at his skin. It snapped in half. We squirreled around backward to look in my broken mirror and laughed, because we were turning ourselves into clowns, into art, into a perfectly matched pair. When we knocked over a beer-bottle pyramid, it would've been better if we weren't sitting on the floor, because not all the bottles were empty and beer ran like a river over the warped wooden floorboards. It ran fast under my leg, over our drawings. I laughed and screamed, jumped up and peeled off my soaked, pastel-smeared jeans.

He took off his pants. Then his boxers, and his cock, first hanging, edged its way up, up, stiffening, to say hello. I pulled off my T-shirt, braless. The windows were open, light pouring in. It was our first time naked together and I had his drawings on my face and he had mine on his body and we saw ourselves in the slice of broken, green-tinged mirror: Adam and Eve, with a pack of crayons.

I pushed the open apartment door closed. *Goodbye, neighbors! Catch you later!*

And he fell on my bed, only a few feet away. I followed.

He climbed on me, skin on skin, warm and ready. Too ready. Right away I felt a splash against my thigh. I looked down, started to ask, "Was that . . . ah?"

He laughed, he apologized, then I laughed too, and he rolled over me, kissed my neck, ran a hand through my long hair—the hair on my head, I mean. But it was only a few minutes before another sploosh hit my leg, this time on my hip. Surprised, I had to stop again, and look at him.

He whispered, "Don't worry, don't worry," and rubbed his cock on my thigh. I thought, okay, now we're getting things going on. But within minutes, there it was—the gush, the geyser. Spew hit my elbow.

For this man, there was no buildup, no way to hold back, and no delay for reloading. He didn't give up. His cock touched my belly, and there was the splash, the sploosh, another pool of splooge. He shot his load like a blind man duck hunting, wildly and at random.

I was a target in some kind of pie-throwing contest, only the pies were more like raw eggs. He couldn't hold his stuff—he tossed come everywhere.

If it's true sperm is good for the skin, I was like at a day spa. If it's really packed with antidepressants, the way some doctors say, then this guy was a walking pharmacy. Once a virgin in Brazil died of anaphylactic shock the first time she had sex, allergic to semen, and thank god that wasn't my problem.

I reached for Kleenex to put on the wet spots, then lay back on the bed. When the spewey puddles got heavy around us, we rolled to the other side of the bed. Too soon we had to move again, to the very edge. Before I was even aroused, we had to move down near the bottom of the bed, the only dry spot left, then over to the floor. And I hadn't even gotten started. It was all him—just shooting and shooting. He tried to go down on me, but his body crumpled, bent in half, as he let his load fly again.

He was a sprinter, a wild hose, a fire extinguisher—and the only fire going out was mine. I couldn't quit counting, quit watching, until I was an observer, not a part of the act. His act. After a while, I got up, left him in his swimming pool, what had been my bed. I went to take a shower.

That might've been the end of our entanglements. He wasn't the man for me. But, right away he hooked up with one of my closest friends. There was a night we were all out on the town, drinking big drinks and looking for trouble. It was early morning when the three of us crashed out in my big bed. It wasn't about sex, it was about sleeping. That's what my friend and I thought, anyway.

I woke up to a familiar sploosh against my thigh. I woke up to a tongue on my clit, a hand on my hip, another splash against my fingers. I reached down, felt his head. Then I sat up fast. I yelled his name. My friend woke up, too. *What the fuck?*

My friend and I, we have our code of ethics. He was her man now. And she was right there, in bed, beside us.

Kerouac, Basquiat, Pollock—what this lovely puppy dog of an artist, this sweet overexcitable man said was, "I thought she was you! I thought you were her!"

My friend and I, we had to send him packing, to kick him out, together.

Abeer Hoque

IN BED WITH SALINGER

Sal and I met in New York about a year ago. We have mutual friends. His best friend and my best friend met at a full-moon party in Thailand. He's working in New York and I'm living in San Francisco, so we didn't see each other again until a week ago, when we showed up at the same Burning Man party somewhere in the middle of Nowhere, Potrero. He was done with his residency and working at a hospital in the Bay Area. I was doing what I always do. Writing sometimes, working less, dancing most.

As with most doctors I know, Sal is happily coexisting with a fairly serious drug habit. For some reason, I find this fact more interesting than troubling. Maybe I have too much faith in medical judgment, or too little in my own.

In any case, I like Sal immediately. He's sweet and silly and sharp, even when fucked up. He has this laugh that's like a little boy's giggle. It gets me. We only kiss that night, in that way that ecstatics do, all love and no urgency. Sal kisses too fast. He tells me later it was probably the coke. Still, I'm not convinced. So when he asks me out for dinner, I hesitate. Plus, I already have plans to stop by a friend's house for drinks. But he persists, so I give him a two-hour slot and make him promise to get me to Aisha's by half past nine.

Dinner is great. Tapas in the Mission. Sal smells good. Looks sharp. Laughs often. I drink my share of an excellent bottle of Syrah.

As promised, he gets me to the Haight by a quarter after nine. I thank him with a kiss, which he returns and I lengthen. I should mention that I lose my mind when it comes to making out in cars. I don't know what it is. Maybe it's because I wasn't allowed to date in high school. Maybe it's the gearshift up my ass. Ten minutes later, we're still in the car, and I ask if he's got a condom. No matter that until ten minutes ago, I had no desire to have sex, let alone with Sal. He doesn't.

"Too bad," I say, with some amount of relief and regret.

"I have some at home," he offers quickly.

"Yeah, but that's not here, or now," I say even quicker.

We kiss some more. He's superhard. I can feel him. Bigger than I expected. Not that that's my thing. It's just that it's nice when it's obvious.

"I'll have you back at Aisha's by eleven," he says, his hand going down my jeans.

"I have my period," I say, wriggling away. It's true.

"I don't care," he says, his hand unwavering in its path.

"Oh . . ." I say, and right there, the deed is done. Signed. We're driving.

Sal lives in a house in Noe Valley owned by a gay couple with six cats. Sal's own cat is the seventh. The eleventh tenant is an alternative nutritionist. I mention a slight cat allergy. He tells me about their rigorous cleaning schedule, the weekly maid, the lack of carpets, and besides, one of the cats is an outdoor cat. Right. That leaves six. We park on a steepish hill and climb the stairs to the house. The front door opens.

"I need to talk to you, Sal," a man says urgently.

"Sure," Sal says easily. "That's Jack," he says to me.

"Alone," the man says abruptly.

"Okay," Sal says, surprised, as he's pulled inside the house. I stand and watch as the door is shut firmly in front of me. I turn around. San Francisco winks and twinkles below me. Perfect, I think. I should have quit while I was in the car. But it's about to get better.

Sal opens the door and exclaims, "One of Jack and Davin's cats is dead."

"Oh, God," I say, feeling a bit petty for my thoughts.

"Come in," he says, disappearing into the house.

The house is gorgeous even in the dark. Sal is in the kitchen listening to Jack speak quickly and brokenly. I can hear snippets of their conversation.

". . . only five years old . . . maybe poison . . . just got home . . . lying on the kitchen floor . . ."

I stand in the dining room, allowing my eyes to adjust. There's a woman standing close by, looking into the kitchen. She must be Summer, the alternative nutritionist.

Summer looks at me. "You shouldn't be here."

You don't know the half of it, I think to myself.

She gets up. "You can wait in the living room," she says, and leads me into a plushly modern room in the front of the house.

I pace the room, wondering if it will take longer to call a cab or catch a Muni bus back to Aisha's.

Sal appears. "They're taking Moses to the vet. His body is still warm. He might still be alive."

"Do you need to go with?" I ask, "Because that's totally cool, if so."

"No," he says with slightly more force than necessary, "Summer's going. And besides, someone has to be home for when Davin gets in."

I stand there uncertainly. I'm not feeling very sexed-up anymore, but Sal is apparently unwilling to give up at this stage. But first he shows me the TV room where they've locked up the other cats, in case Moses ate some poison that's still in the house. Inside are many cats, draped over furniture, stretched out on the floor. As the door swings open, all cat heads turn simultaneously toward us. They remain staring as Sal closes the door. Surreal.

Sal's bedroom is on the small side. It has a slanted roof that's kind of annoying, even if you're average height like me.

But his kisses are slower this time, and I haven't gotten play in a while, so my resistance fades as quickly as he can take off my clothes. I peel off my underwear, trying to hide the white pantiliner stuck on the inside. Luckily, I'm on the tail end of my period, so I'm not about to bleed all over his sheets. But still, I say it. To remind him. "What if I bleed all over your sheets?"

"It can all be washed," he says without hesitation, and heads south.

I don't know any boys who'd do this. I'm touched. And a little paranoid. Okay, a lot paranoid. Enough to know that I'm not going to come easily. Plus a door just banged downstairs. I remember Moses and pull Sal reluctantly away from my clitoris.

Sal isn't a whole lot taller than me, maybe half a foot. Perfect height. But that's probably because I dated someone his height for seven years. My smell isn't very strong on his skin, so I relax. Maybe my period's done after all. He's broad, too, and very strong. His kisses are demanding. I like demanding. Makes me feel less so. I ask about the condoms again. I'm such a sucker. Sex doesn't even make me come, but it's intimate and communal. He leans over me and pulls a condom packet from his bedside table.

"But I don't want to have sex yet," I say, hoping the foreplay isn't already over.

He tosses it aside. I wonder whether he should have put it on anyway. Especially since there are some things I like to do, like rubbing a hard penis against my clit, that makes it difficult for said penis to remain noncoital. Sure enough, soon enough, Sal is inside me.

"Sal, this is unprotected sex," I say.

"I get tested every week," he says, breathlessly, "At the hospital. I'm clean."

Right. And it does feel good. Not orgasmic or anything, but pretty damn good. Sal comes in like a minute. Great. And now there are multiple voices coming from downstairs.

"Where's the bathroom?" I ask, hoping I haven't just gotten myself a UTI.

"Downstairs, by the kitchen."

"You're fucking kidding, right?" I say, feeling wetness beginning to descend inside me.

"Jack and Davin want to put one on the second floor, but they haven't yet. Sorry."

I pull on my clothes in a hurry, shove my underwear into my pocket, and follow Sal downstairs. He stops to have a chat with Summer.

". . . maybe an aneurysm . . ." she's saying, not sparing me a glance.

What is her problem, I wonder as I hurry past and into the kitchen. Maybe she has a thing for Sal? The kitchen is warm and cozy, plants everywhere, but it's the bathroom that's a wonder. Beaded curtains, elevated toilet, sparkling tiles, claw-foot tub. So very fem. I love it. But there's a second door that's open, leading into what is apparently Jack and Davin's bedroom. Jack is lying on the bed.

"Sorry," I say awkwardly, as I shut the door. And I am sorry, for so many reasons.

I kick off my shoes, peel off my jeans and socks, and climb into the tub. I crouch by the faucet and turn on the hot water. From the other room, I can hear Jack start to cry. Blood and come ooze out of me, rushing down the drain. I look up at the ceiling. There are painted stars up there, bright yellow.

Fuck, the water's too hot. But I feel like it will do the trick. You know, the trick of washing away disease. Even though Sal says he's clean. And I even believe him. Either way, I'm going to the city clinic tomorrow. They have drop-in services and anonymous online notification. Classic San Francisco: casual sex and elaborate technology.

The beaded curtains clink against each other, and Jack keeps crying, and crying and crying.

Neal Pollack

MAN'S BEST FRIEND

In the summer of 1995, I learned that my roommate was leaving town. I decided to get my own apartment, but I still needed a companion. Gabby was an ordinary-looking gray tabby, though her mother, attacked by a black tom in an alley rape, had apparently been Siamese. After spending a few minutes with her litter, I determined that Gabby was by far the most amusing.

My first few years with Gabby were a magical textbook of owner-pet symbiosis. There was always another cat around; for a few months, Gabby shared space with my soon-to-be-ex-roommate's cat Sylvie, a dyspeptic, smelly Siamese who liked no one but her owner, and, to everyone's surprise, Gabby, and the two of them became close friends. Gabby was never jealous of the women who, on rare occasions, I brought home. She charmed all she surveyed; she was one of those cats who could be called, in that most backhanded of pet compliments, "like a dog." I concluded that she was the perfect pet, that she, in fact, had magical powers. But then something with Gabby went horribly . . . wrong.

In 1998, I moved in with Regina, the woman who I eventually married. She had two cats of her own, both extremely needy, enormous alpha males. One of those, Growltigger, was an obese sweetheart with a congenital heart defect. He had the terrible habit of excreting a foul-smelling viscous white liquid from his anal glands whenever he became excited, a process that Regina charmingly called "assing," as in, "Ew. Growltigger just assed in my hair."

Although Gabby somehow struck a truce with Regina's monsters, even curling up in their fat folds on especially cold Chicago days, at the same time, she became increasingly attached to me, probably for protection. She developed a habit of draping herself around my shoulders as I wrote at my desk.

One day, Regina said, "Why is Gabby licking your ear?"

"Really?" I said. "I didn't even notice."

"You and that cat," she said. "She's in love with you. It's unnatural."

"Don't be silly," I said.

I still have nocturnal emissions. They've actually tapered off quite a bit in the last two years, but until recently, I often came in my sleep several times a month. In the fall of 2000, Regina and I moved to Philadelphia, for reasons that I still don't quite understand. The incident I'm about to describe took place in our Philadelphia bedroom, illumined by the full moon shining through our skylight.

I was having a sexy dream, the content of which I don't quite recall. But I do remember feeling very warm and full and murmuring "ohhhh," if not out loud, then at least in my mind. Then came release, and a gradual satisfied emerging into consciousness.

Mmmm, I thought to myself.

Wait.

What was that between my legs?

No.

Please, no.

I looked under the covers. There, at my crotch, was Gabby. Oh, sweet God, no! I pulled her out. Gabby's fur was completely slathered with my semen.

My brain filled with equal parts disgust, sadness, and panic. Gabby protested grandly as I ripped her out of the bed by her underside to keep her from touching the covers. I held her in front of me at a careful distance, went into the bathroom, put her on the sink, and locked the door.

Out came a washcloth and soap. I turned on the faucet and started scrubbing. Usually, I'm proud of the fact that I come buckets. It was making this job much more difficult.

After a few minutes, Regina knocked on the door.

"What are you doing in there?" she said.

Gabby mewed in protest.

"Is Gabby in there with you?"

I was a twelve-year-old caught masturbating.

"Go away!" I said.

"Neal," she said. "Open this door right now."

I could no longer live in my private hell, so I let her in.

"What's going on in here?" she said.

My sobbing began quickly and intensely.

"I . . . I . . . I came on Gabby!"

"You what?"

"She was between my legs, and I had a wet dream!"

Then Regina laughed, not just giggling, either, and not kindly. But it wasn't funny to me. Not at all.

Gabby lives with us still. She's still up in my face all the time, wanting to snuggle, to get on my shoulders, to lick my ears. I'm more likely to fling her off than not. The most common thing I say to Gabby now is "leave me the fuck alone, you little bitch!" She loves me anyway, and I feel guilty.

Barely three years later, that night seems like myth. I have to wonder how much Gabby had to do with my orgasm. The best possible scenario, and it's not good, is that I did what I did because her fur was soft. At worst, she instigated the whole affair. Still, regardless of whether or not Gabby gave me a blowjob in Philadelphia, I'm a dog person now.

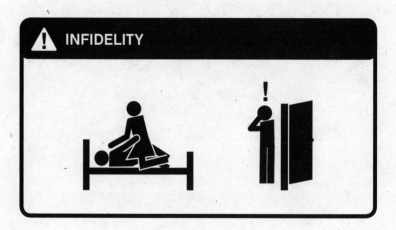

Jonathan Ames

THE FAILED COMB-OVER

Several years ago, when I was in my mid-thirties, I attended a writer's conference at a small Southwestern university. One of the students—not in my class—began to spend time with me. She had just graduated college and was exceedingly lovely, with very long blonde hair that went all the way to her waist. When we would go for walks in the woods near the university all we did was make out, but on the last night of the conference I sneaked her into my room (we didn't want people gossiping). I was in the midst of a drinking relapse—I'm not supposed to imbibe—and was quite intoxicated. We got naked and eventually I put on a condom and tried to get it in her but couldn't. She was very tight and I was very tight (drunk, that is). I had gone down on her, so she was wet enough, but she was too tight, and with all the booze in my system, my erection started to wilt when it wasn't given easy access. Then, somehow, I got my semihard penis in there, and I think my penis was so relieved that it let down its guard, spazzed out, and prematurely ejaculated.

This was terribly embarrassing, so I went down on her again for some time to compensate for my lousy lovemaking and eventually we both fell asleep. She left my room in the wee hours of the morning and when I woke up a little while later and went to the bathroom, I saw that my face was a mask of blood. At first I thought something had happened to me, that I had put my face through a window in my drunkenness, but then I realized that the girl had started her period and when I went down on her the second time my face had gotten covered. I recalled that she had been very wet, but I had thought it was just her natural effusion. Also, the room had been very dark so I hadn't perceived the blood, and in my intoxicated state I hadn't discerned the taste of it. Somewhat disturbed, I washed off the dried blood. What a strange night it had been. I figured she hadn't said anything when she left probably out of embarrassment.

Anyway, the conference broke up later that morning and the girl and I parted sweetly. Naturally, I didn't say anything about her having her period all over my face, and, anyway, I was more embarrassed and upset about my bad lovemaking skills than about her menstruating on me.

About a month later she moved to New York, contacted me, and we ended up in bed. We were naked and just getting into things when she said, "I have something to tell you." I figured she was going to confess to me about having her period that night and that she was sorry she had bled all over me, and so she took a deep breath and then said, "When we had sex a month ago . . . well, I was a virgin. That was my first time. I'm sorry I didn't say anything then."

I was flabbergasted, to say the least. I couldn't believe that her first time had been with a drunken, prematurely ejaculating idiot. I was so embarrassed. Also, she was the first virgin I had ever been with and I hadn't even known it! No wonder she had been so hard to penetrate, and my face, I realized, had been painted with the blood of her broken hymen!

"Why me?" I asked.

"Because you're old, and I figured you would know what to do, and for some reason I got it in my head that I should lose my virginity with someone that I can't have a relationship with."

"Why can't you have a relationship with me?" I asked.

"You're too old for me," she said. "But we can have sex."

That seemed fair enough, and, boy, did I put in a Herculean effort that night to make up for what had transpired a month before, and I have to say, I really redeemed myself. She left late the next morning and about an hour after she was gone the doorbell rang. I went to the front door and it was my ex, who had broken up with me two months earlier and for whom I had been pining (hence the drinking relapse at the conference). But she had finally returned! She came up to my apartment and said, "I've been calling you all night and all morning."

"My phone has been off," I said, which it had been since I was with the other girl. My ex bought this explanation and with hardly another word exchanged between us, she stripped off her clothes. I rallied to the cause and performed admirably. When it was over, we were lying there rather happily, but then she located a very long blonde hair on my pillow. My ex, I should mention, had short black hair.

"What's this?" she said, quite accusingly.

At the time, I had thinning blond hair, which was styled in that classic configuration known as the comb-over. I took the hair from her and said, "It's mine," and I proceeded to drape the hair from my left ear to my right, fitting it in with the other comb-over strands, except the hair kept going—it went from my left ear all the way to my right hip!

"That's why you didn't answer your phone," she shouted. "You had someone here last night! This is disgusting! I think I'm going to throw up!"

She then leaped out of my bed, got dressed faster than I've ever seen a woman dress, and ran out of the apartment and, ultimately, out of my life, and I was heartbroken. I did try racing after her in my slippers that day, but it was futile, as were my subsequent phone calls and pleas.

As a slight compensation, the lovely girl who generously gave me her virginity slept me with me one more time but then found a boyfriend her age and that was that.

(So all the sex in this story was quite good, except that first bloody night, but, ultimately, the results of it all were mostly quite bad.)

Lisa Gabriele
DEAD WOOD

When Christian, the chiseled-jawed, soot-covered, mirrored-sunglass-wearing smoke jumper punched open the swinging doors of the Triple Y Saloon, I had no idea it would soon be over between me and my boyfriend, Ewan, that it would be just a matter of hours before I'd find myself not only single, but homeless, all my belongings tossed out the side of the slow-moving Volkswagen van in which Ewan and I had lived happily for months like fleece-covered Gypsies.

Initially, Ewan had to convince me that Dawson City, Yukon Territory, was a good idea after our not-so-lucrative stint driving cabs in Whistler. But I loved Dawson instantly, loved its weird lonely people, loved the dusty streets, and its garishly painted Victorian homes with the two-by-fours supporting the outside walls. They reminded me of old ladies wearing too much makeup. But as embarrassing as it is to admit, the only thing I loved more than the twenty-four hours of summer daylight was the math of it all. In Dawson it was about nineteen men to every woman, a ratio that had a complicated effect on my moral makeup. If before I was the recipient of the casual male gaze, in Dawson I was a frickin' neon supermodel, a horrible gift to hand to a funny, plain girl with an epic inferiority complex fueled by years of boys picking my blonde willowy friends over me. It was like I had been handed special powers, albeit temporary, geographically specific powers, but ones I'd utterly exhaust nonetheless. Men (always men) would come into town after weeks in the wilderness finding gold, paving roads, or fighting fires, to do what frontier men always did: sleep, bathe, gamble, and fuck. They'd shave off bills from the fat ball of cash and shove them down my costumed bosom. I had regulars who'd slap my ass, whistle my name, and stare at my tits so often that I began to forget it was very wrong for men to treat women like that. While the attention, however sexist, was intoxicating, I never thought I'd act on my flirtations until Christian. But when I watched him clean his soot-encrusted fingernail with a fork, he instantly turned everything I once loved about Ewan into a set of twee ticks.

"Hey beautiful. Listen. We're going to the Midnight Sun later," Christian said, throwing money on the table. "You be there."

"Okay," I said.

It—I—was that easy.

After shift, I said goodbye to Ewan, who was opening the bar, and a friend and I headed to the Sun to penetrate the tough outer corona of women surrounding the smoke jumpers' tables. We felt like sperm wiggling toward the egg. After many drinks and heavy glances my superpowers seemed to be in full force, with the added effect of wiping out all memory of the boyfriend with whom I lived in a van that was our home.

I don't remember how I found myself out back smushed against the dumpster with Christian's hands up the front of my T-shirt, but I know how I ended up back at his hotel room above the Triple Y Saloon. Christian said, "Let's go back to my hotel room above the Triple Y Saloon," to which I replied, "Okay."

We tiptoed across a few streets cursing the tattletale sun, and made a stealthy entrance through the hotel's side door, evading Ewan. Christian blared rock music on both clock radios and ripped off his T-shirt, baring a ludicrously perfect set of abs.

"Let's take off all our clothes and fuck in the shower," he yelled over the Aerosmith.

"Okay," I yelled back.

Many things conspired to ruin the sex, and consequently my life as I knew it then: massive amounts of booze had crippled my judgment and rendered Christian completely flaccid. However, it did not dampen his heroic determination to have sex with me standing up—be damned the assaultive shower water, be damned that the water itself contained neither lubricant nor adhesive properties. It's difficult enough to slip a wet hand into a tight rubber glove, but doing it with boneless fingers is impossible. I felt like I was being hammered against the tiles by a life-size G.I. Joe, who, instead of a penis, was given a small rubber duck we now soundlessly squeezed between us. I understood then how jaws like Christian's become chiseled into those manly, angular shapes. Concentrated masculine determination causes teeth to fiercely clench, neck muscles to deeply spasm, and it turns whomever the guy is fucking into a mission that requires accomplishment. Christian's handsome face seemed to be saying: Must get my dick in that hole there. Must get it in that. In. Get in. He wasn't a regular firefighter after all. This was a man who jumped out of low-flying planes in order to arrive AT the fire.

I was no help. I was too busy trying to prevent permanent paralysis—surely the result of us falling backward, snapping my spine in two over the lip of the slippery tub. But mostly what wrecked the sex was knowing that my boyfriend was a few feet below while I betrayed him—something that played havoc with the four or five cells still fiercely squatting in my conscience.

In my drunkenness, I had pulled down the shower rod, dispensing with the bothersome curtain altogether. I was trying to be sexily destructive, but the Triple Y was not a historic structure. Rather, its false front saloon exterior hid four stacked prefab boxes, walls and floors made of Styrofoam. While Christian redoubled his efforts, the ceiling below us hung pregnant with shower water. After it burst all over the drunken patrons and their cuckolded bartender, the night-desk girl ran upstairs to bang on the door. The water and the Foreigner drowned her out so she begged Ewan to take an axe to the door. While many people saw me naked for the first time ever that night, for Ewan it was the last. The next day, from the window of the jewelry store, I watched as he tossed my things out of the van and onto the dusty sidewalk. I don't remember if I waved as he drove out of Dawson City for good, but I do remember I had been standing, my battered pussy as clean as it would ever be that summer.

Kevin Keck

INTERLUDE WITH THE VAMPIRE

I was sitting in the sun trying to collect my thoughts before I taught my next class. Things had not been going well, and I had the constant feeling that I needed to take a nap.

My fatigue was a product of my girlfriend's temper. Her sexual talents were such that it was easy to overlook her weekly fits of alcohol-induced rage: a broken television, smashed glasses, personal items dismissed from the apartment via the window.

In retrospect, the solution was simple: change the locks and quit answering her calls. However, as much as I hate to admit it, I was genuinely afraid of this woman, and not because of the threat she posed to my more fragile possessions: she routinely smacked the shit out of me. Because of my slight build, I learned early in life to extract myself from volatile situations with a quick wit or, failing that, a pretty quick sprint. Such tactics are fairly useless against an angry woman, as I discovered when Lorraine began ranting at me one night when I attended a poetry reading without her:

"I know you're just out trying to fuck someone else!" She whipped a book at my head. Luckily it was *Gravity's Rainbow*, which is not at all aerodynamic. "Some fucking poetry slut!" (Oh, if only such a slut did exist!)

I bore the constant humiliation of my girlfriend slapping me around in my typical manner: I got stoned. Whatever the drawbacks of marijuana, it's good for helping one forget the recent past. Alas, one of those drawbacks is that being high and being angry cannot occur simultaneously. During the days, though, I stewed with venom. I thought of men like Robert Mitchum, Humphrey Bogart. They weren't violent toward women, but by God, when a woman needed straightening out, they didn't hesitate to give her a solid slap. Sometimes two, if the occasion warranted. I dreamt often of slapping Lorraine so hard it would knock her earrings off. However, the fact that I wanted my slap to be an homage to June Allyson's bitch-slap of Joan Collins in *The Opposite Sex* gave me the impression that I was not the man for the task.

All of this was swimming in my head when one of my students sat down beside me and said:

"So, you ever had any absinthe before?"

The comment wasn't completely random. Gary was a student in my American literature class, and during a lecture on Hemingway I was prompted to explain a reference to absinthe

in a short story. He'd been the only other person in the room
who knew what it was.

I told him a friend had brought some back from Europe
several years before, and I'd tried it then.

"Did it fuck you up?" His tone lacked the voyeurism of
indulgence one might expect; it had a palpable clinical nature
to it.

"I didn't have enough."

"Well, if you ever want some, let me know; I keep it
around."

"You like it that much?"

"No, it's . . . " Gary took a drag from his cigarette and
glanced around; we were more or less alone. "I practice vam-
pirism. It's part of a ritual."

I turned my head toward Gary: he was a stocky country
boy with coal-black hair and muscles shaped by labor and not
the ridiculous repetition of weights; he looked directly into my
eyes, and his eyes were the color of slate. I'd gotten used to
students telling me completely bizarre and personal things—
people are always looking for an authority figure to heap their
issues on for some shred of absolution. And even though this
was quite possibly in the top three weirdo admissions of all
time, I thought it best not to laugh at his confession. But it was
hard to ignore the fact that I was sitting directly under the sun
with a guy who claimed to be a vampire.

"So what's with the absinthe?" I asked.

"Oh, that. Well, you know it's potent shit. Most people it just fucks up. But it won't even intoxicate a vampire. It's a test, you know. To see if you've got the gene."

"What gene?"

"The vampire gene."

A scientific debate with someone claiming the existence of a vampire gene seemed rather pointless. I let the matter slide.

"So, do you like, you know, bite necks?"

"Do I look like I have fucking fangs to you?" He flashed his teeth.

"Uh, no."

"Yeah," and his face dropped. "It sucks. I just can't afford to have the work done. You'll meet people tonight who've got them. Some are quality dental work. Some just look like shit because people file their teeth—that's just fucked up. Some people just get lucky by birth. But if I could afford them, I'd have them."

I wasn't sure how to respond to this, so I sat quietly. Then Gary said:

"How old do I look to you?"

"I don't know," I said. "Twenty-five?"

"I'm thirty-eight."

"You're older than me."

"Get yourself a woman who treats you right. You'll feel the difference in your blood." He smiled, exposing a mouthful of beautiful white teeth. "Just think about it. If you want to meet a nice girl, I know the place." I wasn't sure what a vampire who attended the local community college might have in mind when he said "nice girl," but considering my own circumstances at the time, I didn't need to bring any more drama into my life.

When I got home that night, I made the puzzling discovery that my apartment was littered with confetti. Upon closer examination I realized the confetti was actually the pages of my journals, which Lorraine had taken great care to manufacture into fantastically small pieces. Apparently, my private thoughts about her were not to her liking. I found a note in the bathroom that read: *Fuck you!* I also found my toothbrush in the toilet.

The next day after class I asked Gary just what he meant by a "nice girl."

"Come and see for yourself. I'm going there tonight."

"Where?"

"Purgatory."

I considered this. "On a Tuesday?"

I met Gary (or rather, Count Gary, as I'd begun to think of him) later that night outside the bar that hosts Purgatory. I'd researched it a little on the Internet that afternoon—it was a monthly gathering of the leather and BDSM communities. It seemed safe enough, but whenever someone admits to being a vampire and then invites you to attend a place called Purgatory with them, well, I feel a background check is in order.

As we walked in, Gary put his arm around my shoulder and said, "Tonight you'll feel like a new man." The leather of his jacket creaked in my ear.

In my daily existence, I am most often dressed like a nine-year-old on his way to baseball practice: Converse sneakers, jeans, and a jersey-style T-shirt with three-quarter-length sleeves. However, I was surrounded by extras from *Interview with the Vampire* or a Renaissance festival. I felt like the Southern preppy in Count Gary's court.

My mood might have tepidly approached something close to genuine fear had we been in a place more "dungeon-esque." However, we were at a bar known for its regular booking of tribute bands, and a leather-clad person with honest-to-God fangs doesn't look that threatening in front of a sign advertising two-for-one Jell-O shooters and $1.50 margaritas on Fridays.

After we'd paid our $10 cover (it seemed only fitting one should pay a nominal fee to gain entrance to Purgatory), I followed Gary to the bar and ordered the best beer available—a Corona, for Christ's sake! Oh, Purgatory indeed! I discreetly popped two Percocets in my mouth, crunched them up, and washed them down.

Gary stood at such a distance from me that it was uncertain as to whether we actually knew each other or not. I sat on a bar stool and waited for the warm bliss of the Percs to wash over me, and watched as the medievally clad crowd circulated and exchanged greetings. Whenever anyone saw Gary they gave an enthusiastic wave. His reply was a terse nod in every case. Whenever their eyes fell on me they all appeared to snarl. I smiled politely and raised my Corona.

This went on for some time, and because no one was speaking to me—including Gary—I was soon tipping back my fifth Corona and considering a cab ride home. The Nine Inch Nails that had been pumping on the stereo since our arrival had given way to something resembling the sounds of a genocidal massacre mixed with asphalt production, and it was decidedly not conversation friendly. The scene seemed a terrible waste of a buzz, and I felt as though I were literally buzzing. Humming, in fact.

A petite girl with purple streaks in her hair and ample piercings walked over to Gary and curtsied. He smiled at her and opened his arms; when he embraced her he pressed his face into her neck. She was wearing a thin black dress, dog collar, and a pair of bright white Keds that glowed under the black lights. Gary yelled at the girl, "This is my friend, Kevin." The veins in his neck stood out, but he was still barely audible over the music. I leaned my head close to theirs.

"Heaven?" she said.

"Kevin," Gary repeated.

"Oh." She turned to me and smiled and curtsied again.

Gary pressed his lips to my ear. "Okay, you're all set. I've got business to take care of. I'll see you later. Or maybe not." He gave me what I can only characterize as a wicked smile. I grabbed his arm before he could walk away.

"What? Where are you going?"

"I'm going to find something to eat. Amanda is yours for the night. I set it all up. She'll treat you right. Remember that when you're grading finals." Gary winked.

"How do you know her?"

He smiled at me again: "She's a good source of food." I let go of his arm and he pressed into the crowd.

As soon as he was gone I said to Amanda, "Can I buy you a drink?"

"I don't drink." She had the most wonderful dimples when she smiled, and a shy way of looking down. I almost missed it because of the piercings.

"You don't drink? My God, how do you stand it?"

That bashful smile again. "I try to keep my body clean for others."

"Really? You looked like a dirty girl to me." It was my turn to smile. Oh yes: I was flowing with the buzz, reaching into my bag of tricks. In the glow of neon beer signs it was hard to tell if she was blushing. She looked me dead in the eye:

"When you fuck me, choke me."

This was far outside the scope of my bag of tricks. I smiled politely at her and flagged the bartender to bring me another Corona. I downed it quickly as Amanda and I smiled at each other. Occasionally she leaned into me and seemed to say something, but I couldn't hear a fucking word over the music. I smiled and nodded, and that seemed to be working fine. When I was done with my beer I jerked my thumb toward the door, and she and I walked out into the warm night.

"So what's the plan, Amanda?"

"What do you want it to be?" She didn't say it with the flirtatious sarcasm of a sorority girl, but with the submissive tone of someone who genuinely wants to please.

"Well, you mentioned the matter of choking . . ." The way I said it sounded oddly Victorian, but regardless I felt the signs were pretty clear: Gary had set this up, she knew the deal, and it seemed stupid to stand around acting as though the night wasn't going to end up like this anyway. At least once or twice in my life I've stumbled into easy hookups like this and been smart enough to latch on. Conversely, I've managed to fuck things up about two dozen times or more. Probably more. I try not to dwell on superlatives in matters of failure.

Her impish smile blossomed into fierce seriousness. "You can do what you want with me, but do it hard, and drink me up."

As hammered as I was, I recall thinking: *Do people really talk like this?* But then I remembered the scene inside—the goth aesthetic, all the people who clearly thought the Gimp was the best character in *Pulp Fiction*. At this point, everything was beginning to seem like a dream. This little girl standing in front of me was begging to be hurt, and I wanted to hurt someone just as badly as I'd been hurting lately.

"Well, Amanda—" the thought passed through my head that this girl and my mother shared the same name "where are you parked?"

Curiously, her apartment did not bear the stony cold-
ness of a bourgeois succubus's lair, decked out in crystals and
dragons and fairies, but appeared instead to be a showroom for
Pier 1; she had an amazing collection of throw pillows.

As soon as we were in the door she was on me: she was
small, maybe a hundred pounds, and it felt effortless to have
her clinging to me, legs wrapped around my waist. Normally I
don't feel very manly when fucking a woman, more like a beetle
clinging to a lioness. But her tiny body made me feel enormous.
I could have crushed her. We fell among the throw pillows, her
hands working my clothes off with professional ease. As her
tongue worked its way into my mouth, I felt not one, but two,
studs in her tongue. Oh, sweet bliss! I nearly came right then.

She hiked up her dress and said, "Spank my ass."

I complied with her request. I was never one to turn
down a little ass chapping. But with each smack of my hand she
said, "Harder!" Within a few swats my hand was hurting—it
reminded me of playing baseball as a kid, the way the wooden
bat stung your hands and wrists when it connected with the ball.
I reached up and grabbed the dog collar from behind, yanking
backward as her teeth latched onto my lips; I pulled harder and
she came loose from me, splitting my lower lip as she did so.

"Fucking goddamn!" I said.

She ran her tongue across her lips and smiled. That's
when I caught a good glimpse of the fangs. Before I could say
anything, she said: "Wait right here."

The warning signals in my brain were at DefCon 2: *Get the fuck out of here.* But I had lapsed into an opiated euphoria, and I began to imagine her as my vampish girlfriend and how her throw pillows and accent rugs would blend seamlessly into my own apartment and my menagerie of colored glass votives. And Lorraine—she'd quit fucking with me if I had a new girlfriend with fangs.

"I've brought you something special." I opened my eyes; Amanda was holding out a drink to me; her other hand held a shimmering light, and when I sat up to take the drink I saw it was a knife.

Well, so this is how it ends, I thought. I don't know if I was completely twisted or what, but I felt unusually calm—all my problems were about to disappear as I became the victim of some serial killer. It was really quite liberating.

Then she handed the knife to me.

"You don't have to be gentle," she said. She began to peel off her clothing. On one wrist I saw the single tattoo of a razor blade. On the other wrist, the tattoo read "cut here"; the words floated above a dotted line. A mummified kitten was stenciled onto her stomach and chest (I found this somewhat charming as I own cats, and I had to repress the urge to say, "Oh, a little kitty . . ."). She sat beside me on the couch, kissing me with that slight bite, and guided my hand with the knife toward her thigh.

I've never been much for blood—mine or anyone else's. As a child, my annual physicals were something of a nightmare for all involved, as I was (and remain) quick to faint at the sight of a needle or blood being drawn. Even a visit to the dentist presents serious obstacles. Novocain not only numbs me, it puts me into a coma.

"Taste me," she breathed, and I felt her hand pressing against mine, guiding the knife lightly along her leg. I could feel the blackness beginning, as if a pinhole had opened in the back of my head letting all the anger and resentment I'd been hoarding about the circumstances of my life float into the night.

When I came around from the vampiress's sweet embrace, I woke to sunlight. I was sitting on the couch, fully clothed. No one seemed to be in the apartment but me. Had I fallen asleep and only dreamed a meeting with a vampire? Be it so, if you will; I didn't stick around to find out. I made a hasty exit and found my car. When I looked in the rear-view mirror, I saw the cuts on my lower lip.

It occurred to me that Lorraine would have driven by my apartment last night; she would have noticed my absent car, perhaps even waited for me. I could not begin to guess what loss I was about to return to, but I felt it prudent to stop on the way home and purchase a new toothbrush.

ON THE REBOUND

Ari Cohen
BIG TROUBLE

You could say that the bad sex began a year earlier, at the Zurich airport, when I hopped two connecting flights, three subways, and a cab to visit the love of my life in Cambridge, Massachusetts. He met me at his door, and unceremoniously cut the cord. His face was blank, the way men's are when they've already detached and are pretending they don't know you. I took my suitcases and left. We never talked again.

I was a wee bit upset. The chronic nausea lasted a month; the chest pain six. I blasted scorned Stevie Nicks on repeat until people complained. I read *The Noonday Demon: An Atlas of Depression*, 576 pages, cover to cover.

Reader, if I could go back in time, I would have solicited the rebound sex right there and then on that unfortunate day in Cambridge. I would hurl myself onto the cobblestone sidewalk with the first man to cross my path. But I was young and dumb and unaware that cock can be a magic wand of emotional healing. I also thought myself the well-behaved sort of girl who didn't do sex with people she wasn't in love with. Yet I was too battered for another relationship. So instead I just hurt. For a year. Some days I couldn't breathe. I got a job in Asia, didn't meet anyone I liked, and came back. I had no idea that liking had nothing to do with it.

It was during a crying jag a full year later that I realized that maybe, just maybe, I needed to fuck someone else. Brilliant!

Cue Noah: Twenty-four hours after setting my sights on my new career aspiration *(sleep with someone-fucking-else)*, a six-four Kentucky boy named Noah swam into my clutches at a hole called Fish Bar. His face and body inexplicably reminded me of one of those deluxe bags of dry dog food. You know, meaty and too big to lift. But big men have a sort of free pass in the world of mating: they're sexy by the sheer fact that they're big. Few, if any of them, are actually cute in their facial features. But most are normal looking, and they have huge hands that can wrap around your entire waist, and wide broad chests that envelop you and make you feel petite and sexy and safe no matter how not-petite you are, and, in every case I've seen thus far, reasonable endowment. Even if they're small for their size, they're still fine. And they have thick bodies and meaty lips that you can tussle with. I was expecting a good time.

Noah drummed his cork-size fingers to whatever music was playing. Our first five-hour date ended with two A.M. pizza, and, in the following days, I ignored all signs that something was fishy: that he rescheduled our movie date three times due to an apparent inability to function on weekends; that despite this, he was not in therapy or on medication; that when I arrived for our movie date, his apartment was one big pile of pizza boxes, laundry, and shoes. It became clear that he was a good-hearted, dry-witted guy with a newspaper full of mental issues, head-lined by one parent with late-stage Hodgkin's and another with late-stage AIDS. But I was on a mission, and male mental func-tionality wasn't a big part of it.

When Noah finally pulled it together for date Number Two—which I conveniently scheduled about six yards from his bed, in his living room—he ogled my breasts, which I took as a good sign. I was bursting out of an American Apparel top advertised on a nearby semipornographic billboard, combined with a bra so uplifting that I couldn't lean over. We ordered dinner and made small talk over beer about his miserable job at a nonprofit and my awesome life as a writer. I directed the conversation to happy topics: We'd both slept all day, him skipping work altogether, and me because I could. Appar-ently Noah thought that "let's watch a movie at your house" meant that I actually wanted to watch a movie. Silly boy. It was *The Wedding Singer*. My clothes were off before Sandler's opening ditty.

We laid on his couch, me on top of his chest in a bra and itchy-but-hot thong, his enormous hands rubbing my back palm-first, the way you might absentmindedly pet a poodle, not *feeling* anything. This was the first indication that maybe this wouldn't be the best sex ever. Noah wasn't quite mentally functioning enough to have a sense of touch. But my mind said, *I'm sleeping with someone else! I'm sleeping with someone else! Go me!* An enormous erection pressed against my leg. I copped a feel. He was big—errrr, huge, comparable in size to my snazzy new portable phone. My hopes sank. The trouble with well-endowed men is that they tend to have a very limited skill set beyond straight fucking, and Noah's Making Out 101 skills were already deficient. This did not bode well. Basic touching, not to mention oral sex, are not strategies of the well endowed. You will never get an erotic massage from a well-endowed man. The large-cocked among us feel that they don't have anything to prove, which in the domain of the male ego is bad news. They think that they are doing you a favor by offering you their dick, unaware that stores sell similar products in silicone and plastic. My ideal man is reasonably sized, but worried that he's small, and thereby offers a full menu of additional services.

But I figured I'd give Noah the benefit of the doubt. We'd never hooked up before, so I gave us a while to kiss and figure out the other's rhythms. I tried to get into it—passion!— while his enormous hands pawed my back, sort of grabbing at the flesh and letting go. Every minute or so, he stuffed his entire enormous wet tongue into my mouth. The first time I laughed, thinking he was displaying horrendous technique with irony. He wasn't kidding.

But as the pawing and tongue-stuffing continued for twenty minutes, with Noah growing increasingly sweaty, I grew concerned. Noah appeared to have *no sense of touch what-soever*. I know, you think you've slept with someone with no sense of touch. But you haven't. What you experienced was a not-particularly-acute sense of touch. Noah, quite literally, seemed only able to feel inanimate objects. He got my bra off, and stopped moving while he held it in his hand, looking at it, the way one studies a bag of chips at the store. When he seemed satisfied, his wet hands grabbed chunks of my hair, not to pull on it in a sexy way, but to study the consistency of it (Jewish, frizzy). When his body remembered that I was there, his hands were like softball mitts, nudging at me the way one moves around the raw Thanksgiving turkey.

I looked for his other skills. He revealed holey gray boxers, further proof that he hadn't expected me to show up and strip. He periodically shifted, introducing some dry fuck-ing action at a rhythm that had no correlation with what I was doing, and not remotely aligned—he was humping the outside of my right thigh. I paused there, with my head right above his, pressing my lips together to avoid another tongue invasion. He awkwardly patted my back, and then kind of bumped me on the head with his hand, an awkward love pat. That was when I realized I was lying on top of a man with *no sense of touch what-soever. None.* I reconsidered my aspirations. But no. I needed to stay the course! I focused on the good news about Noah: his apartment was so horrifically intolerable by female standards that clearly no one was sleeping with him, and he probably wasn't the walking STD that most of Manhattan can be.

I suggested that we move into the bedroom. He looked surprised. I stifled the urge to announce, *"Dumbfuck, you're going to get laid. I'm rebounding."* His sheets were in a twisted pile falling off the bed. I told myself that they were freshly laundered, and hopped in.

I want you all to be clear that the next forty minutes were truly the lowest in my entire life. Yet they were somehow utterly necessary. Every girl has that one sexual encounter that she doesn't tell anyone about. My friend calls it "the fat fuck." It's like the time I made out with the ugly guy in my high school because I felt I needed practice. In adult world, Noah was my fat fuck.

Noah whipped his fully erect dick out immediately, and condomed up. His dexterity and swiftness in this act were surprising, indicating that perhaps he'd done it before. This gave me hope. He nudged me flat, onto my stomach. I pulled myself up, and he pawed me back down again. Apparently, he wanted me down. It briefly occurred to me that I was alone in the bedroom of an oafy guy I didn't know at all, who had *no sense of touch*. Was he psychotic? I looked at the piles of dirty clothes blocking the closet. Many signs pointed to yes. But no, I'd talked to him for five hours. Noah was just lacking the most pivotal of the five senses, touch. I didn't have time to consider this because he entered me from behind with the force of a tractor-trailer. Just like parties, a slow, fashionably late entrance is always preferable. He'd barged in before the party started. Ow.

I grimaced until it stopped hurting. I attempted to find us a rhythm, but there wasn't one. Nothing. He plunged away with the same attention that one might use when plunging a toilet. None. He heavily pawed at my back, or grabbed a chunk of my ass, oblivious to the fact that I wasn't a pillow. I felt dripping on my back, and turned around to glance a big droplet of sweat dripping from his nose to my back. I turned back around. Luckily, I am blessed with one of those bodies that finds damn near anything pleasurable, and for a few minutes, enjoyed myself and climaxed.

He was still plunging. And plunging. I attempted to sit up, and he pushed me down. I turned around, and noted that he was dripping in sweat, his lightly hairy chest wet, his muscular legs glistening, eyes closed in extremely vigorous effort. I contemplated the fastest way out of this situation. I figured I'd stay put and let him finish.

Five minutes later, nothing had happened. I tried honesty. "Babe, are you by chance on any meds?"

"Nope."

"Oh. Let's try a different position." I flipped onto my back. He reentered, now supporting himself on his arms, dripping all over me, groaning with the effort. I shifted my pelvis downward, minimizing the impact. His eyes were closed, his body rigid and somehow turned off, not feeling anything at all. I could have morphed into the Pillsbury Doughboy, and he wouldn't have noticed.

Upstairs, I heard rhythmic banging. Could they be fucking too? I inquired. "They're toddlers. They play," Noah groaned. Awww, how cute. I closed my eyes and tried to pretend that I was one of the small children thudding into upstairs walls.

I studied him. He was truly oblivious to my presence. I had had some awkward college hookups, where I sensed that my partner was fantasizing about someone else. But this was unprecedented, a whole new level of disconnect. His eyes were closed and his forehead scrunched, looking angry, as if it were straining to feel. I was being fucked by a human ball of emotional tension that couldn't feel a damn thing.

We were quickly shifting from neutral to nonpleasurable to painful. I opened my eyes and looked at the 230-pound body above me. I sent him orgasm karma. *Come on come on come on.* Nothing. I wondered if he was gay—the previous stomach sex had definitely had a whiff of *Brokeback* to it. I decided no. I spoke up. "Is there anything I can do to help?"

"Just . . . give me one . . . more . . ." Nothing. This man was taking his entire emotional past out on my body. I used my body abandonment skills, honed through years of competitive swimming training, where you calmly breathe in and out of your mouth, close your eyes, and stop feeling your body. I came back.

Finally I said it. "OUCH."

He paused. He pulled out and stood up, and opened the bedroom door.

"Where you going?"

"The shower. I need to, um, relax. Get back to zero."

I rolled onto the other side of the bed, away from his sweat stains, and wrapped myself in a dry sheet, grateful that I was no longer being pounded. I shut my eyes, dozing. There is something therapeutic in sleeping with someone who is so obviously more fucked up than you are. Noah returned, a different kind of wet, and wrapped in a towel.

"Um, what are you doing?"

"Resting."

"Oh."

He climbed in bed with me, in a sort of retarded form of spooning, him roughly patting my back.

"Um, do you want to talk about that?"

"I'm just a bit tense."

I got up and went first to the bathroom, then to the kitchen for a glass of water, thoroughly searching the cabinets for signs of antidepressants. Nothing. I returned to bed.

He sat up. "I need to go to sleep now."

This I couldn't believe. Throwing a woman out after sex is bad, but throwing a woman out after *bad sex*—bad, painful, no-sense-of-touch! sex—that's a sin. But I was feeling vulnerable, in that postsex way where you pull into yourself and become passive, so I said okay. I pulled on my hoochie shirt and jeans, and peered out the window. It was blizzarding. Four inches of snow had appeared during my rebound sex, the heavens' way of covering my tracks. The brick window across the way reminded me of Cambridge. He looked out. "Man, it's really snowing." He didn't say anything else.

We hugged, and he delivered one more tongue invasion. I walked down the building's stairs, wet with gray puddles of melted snow. In the lobby, I opened my deluxe umbrella.

Outside, smokers huddled in the doorway of the adjacent bar. I wondered if they could tell that I'd just gotten laid. They didn't seem to notice. I didn't have time to contemplate that thought. As I turned the corner, a gust of wind blew my umbrella to the side, and I stepped onto a patch of ice, landing hard on my ass.

Jen Kirkman

SEDUCED BY *FRASIER*

Daniel was in my writers' group. My friend Anna put the group together to help a bunch of us stay creative. A weekend warrior only, Daniel's real job was computer programming or something like that. His pager and cell phone were clumsily clipped to his braided belt at all times.

I was freshly dumped and had lost sex-with-my-ex privileges after one "this doesn't mean anything" romp ended with me crying when it was time to go home.

The idea was that this writers' group would present me with a rebound man, but Daniel was the only dude there. The sight of the coarse blond hair on his toes that peeked out from his Birkenstocks made me instinctively cross my legs in self-defense. Whenever anyone read their short story out loud, Daniel drew the attention to himself by laughing forcefully, slamming the table with his hand, and moaning, "Ohhh, *God* that's good." He usually threw his head back and made a face that looked like he was taking a bullet in the back or having an orgasm.

Group meetings usually devolved into all of us heading to a bar. Daniel always bought the round of drinks because he was the only one with an expense account. When he was out of earshot, Anna teased, "Doesn't Daniel look like he's about to . . . you know . . . when he laughs at a story?" We all "eww'd" in agreement. Daniel joined us at the table. For every pint of beer he had, he chugged a pint of water, smacked his lips, and wiped the dribble on his chin. He was so orderly and anal with his hydration ratio theories, but he was also caveman-ish, talking with his mouth full of peanuts.

I went home that night a little drunk and alone. A *Frasier* rerun kept me company. Before long I was masturbating on the couch. I want to be clear: I was not touching myself to *Frasier.* It was just on in the background. High off my own love buzz, I watched another episode. There was something weirdly sexy about Kelsey Grammer's character. He was charmingly preten- tious but also loudmouthed and ill at ease, sort of like Daniel. Frasier's bed looked so cozy and inviting. He probably had six- hundred-plus thread-count sheets. And he had the decency to cover up his middle-aged paunch and hairy chest with a smart velvet smoking jacket. I was buzzed enough to masturbate again, this time intentionally to Frasier Crane.

A few nights later the writers' group met at Daniel's apartment, and there was wine. I was impressed that Daniel had bookshelves, not crates; a king-size bed, not a futon. When

Daniel uncorked another bottle of wine, he didn't have to balance the bottle on the counter, and I detected the slightest hint of a muscle on his right arm. His pager and cell phone were on the table, not on his belt, and he was shuffling around in sheepskin slippers. Normally I'd cringe at how showily Daniel put his nose in his wineglass before tasting it, but I decided to overlook it. He was oddly Frasier-esque.

When the rest of the group decided to call it a night, no one looked twice when I announced that I was too tipsy to drive home and that I planned to hang back. Daniel led me toward his bedroom to show me his music collection. I'd feared that he was a Dave Matthews Band kind of guy, but he pulled out Dylan's *Blonde on Blonde* on vinyl and played "Visions of Johanna." I braced myself for his kiss and felt a rush of creepy adrenaline, thinking, "The rest of the group can never know about this." Instead of a kiss, Daniel told me his ten-point plan to retire by age forty-five. I made it easy for him. I lay down on his bed and said, "Can I crash here tonight?" He said, "Sure!"

Daniel went into the bathroom to change and returned wearing a velvet smoking jacket. I blushed, thinking that somehow he'd found me out. His legs were pasty and stocky, and the jacket belt was tied underneath his round belly.

My libido was mad at me for putting it through this.

But perhaps Daniel was going to be good sex, I thought. Since women probably rejected him constantly, maybe he would be the type of guy who would really try to earn my orgasm.

Daniel approached the bed, turned down the lights, and whispered, "I'm going to make myself more comfortable." I wasn't sure if he was trying to be funny, so I giggled to be polite. He stroked my cheek and asked, "Nervous?" I forgave his innocent and patronizing question because his touch actually felt nice.

I let my head fall back as he kissed my neck. This was going exactly as planned. And then Daniel jumped up. "Music! We need music!" He put on more Dylan (a CD this time) and ran back to the bed acting like an animal; not an animal that would devour me sexually, but an animal that might need to be put down, like a rabid raccoon.

Daniel rubbed me everywhere using both hands, causing so much friction I thought I might catch fire. I let him tire himself out a little until finally we found ourselves entwined, which wasn't so bad. It was nice to have a man hold me again. And then I felt his toenail in my calf. Ouch. Gross. Unwind my leg. Daniel grinned above me and asked, "Are you ready?" I was ready, and in a forgiving mood.

Daniel pulled a condom out from under his pillow and rolled it on. He kept looking at his penis, then back at me. I wondered if he wanted some congratulations.

As he climbed on top of me, I feared I might laugh once he was inside. But he was slow, and there was an actual spark of intimacy between us during the first few seconds of "intercourse," as Daniel called it. Then he began to narrate, just as obviously as he did in his pulp sci-fi stories. "Uh . . . we're doin' it. Yeah. Yeah." His eyes were squeezed shut, and I grabbed him tightly to try to shut him up. This caused him to narrate louder. "Oh yeah! You are so passionate when we do it."

In my mind, I downgraded this from sex to what I call "masturbation-with-help." I closed my eyes and pictured my guilty pleasure of the moment, Frasier Crane. With my eyes shut I didn't notice that Daniel had used his CD player remote to turn up the music. We were actually going at it to the song "Hurricane." Bob Dylan sang, "Don't forget that you are white." I said, "Daniel. Can we turn this song off?"

But it was too late. As the violins crescendoed into chaos, so did Daniel. And then I heard a familiar groan: "Oh . . . that's good." He made the face. He looked like he was taking a bullet in the back and wailing loudly at the gods for destroying his city. Daniel smiled like a goofball at me, and I feared he'd just fallen in love. "Jen, we can never tell the writers' group about this," holding up his pinky finger in solidarity. A pinky swear? I was the one who should be denying *him* permission to tell. "Don't you think part of the fun is that no one knows we're doing this?" he asked.

I'd sobered up considerably and drove home soon after. When I was back on my couch, I turned on the TV and was taunted by the familiar theme song. I talked back to the TV. "I was just horny, you know," I told Frasier. "To be honest, you gross me out. I didn't mean to fantasize about you. I'm rebounding!" And with that, Frasier took his next call and said, "I'm listening."

Jami Attenberg

GETTING DOWN WITH OCD

The first time Peter asked me if I had been tested for sexually transmitted diseases was over dinner, on our first date. He casually slid the question into conversation just as one might ask the name of your hometown or if your parents were still married. I can't even remember if he actually asked me or just mentioned it, so practiced was he at extracting the information. I only remember that I was soon admitting that I had been tested one month previously, and I was clean as a whistle—a whistle that had never been sucked or touched or placed in inappropriate locations.

I did find it strange that he asked about it over dinner (a crab-cake sandwich for me, a hearty soup for him), but these are modern times, my friends, and we all wonder about a potential partner's baggage, both physical and emotional. Maybe it was even refreshing, I thought, his forthrightness. Usually those questions are asked in the moments before penetration, as a condom waits to be hurriedly stretched down the length of a penis. A whisper in the ear: "Are you clean?" "Are you healthy?" "Is there anything I should know?" These are all times when decision-making and truth-telling abilities are limited. But he was planning ahead. He was a planner. I could learn to like that.

After dinner we went to a dot-com party, one of the approximately ninety being thrown on any given Thursday during the year 2000, and walked in together as some sort of semblance of a couple. Peter and I were both Web producers, though on the opposite end of the spectrum: I worked on entertainment Web sites, and he worked for financial-planning institutions. We were both on the same party circuit, and we had little in common besides our workaholic tendencies. He was really into experimental jazz and enjoyed long and thought-ful discussions about politics; I liked Sleater-Kinney and making fun of strangers. He was well mannered and chival-rous and always went home alone. I drank a lot and was in a phase of my life (e.g., my twenties) where I fucked men as if the phrase "use it or lose it" had been invented specifically for my vagina. But time and again I had found myself talking to him at these parties. We both always stayed till the end, me to drink myself silly, and Peter, I suppose, to keep himself from feeling alone.

A week before, we had made out after one of these same parties, hurriedly on a bench outside of a bar in Chelsea. He had blatantly stroked my breasts in full view of everyone walking by on the street, and it had felt so good I hadn't cared that I was a terrible, awful cliché. I could feel part of me moving outside of my body and seeing myself doing it, how I must have looked like that girl, getting felt up at two A.M. It was not a finer moment, but the attention had buoyed me, he had started it, and then, suddenly he stopped, and announced he was going to go home and jerk off. To my great surprise, he e-mailed me the next day and asked me to dinner. This was something new and fascinating: a guy who wanted to date me.

And now here we were, this new version of us, different than the week before. He was gracious and attentive. He got me free drink after free drink from the open bar, and did the same for all of my friends who were there. He told his serious and sincere stories about his life and family and travels, and they suddenly seemed sparkling to me. We smiled at each other across the room when we thought no one was looking. I'm totally going to fuck him later, I thought.

We went back to his apartment (spotless, unsurprisingly), and we sat and he asked me more questions about myself, my strengths, my weaknesses, my dreams. He rubbed my feet as we talked. There was the fiercest radiation between us. It felt like something was happening. And then he said, "So I think we're probably going to have sex at some point, so I have to ask you, have you been tested for sexually transmitted diseases?"

Perhaps I hadn't been clear enough at dinner, I thought. Perhaps he wants more details. I launched into a longer explanation, and added in a funny anecdote about my visit to the gynecologist (some sort of *Vagina Monologues* joke while she was investigating me with a speculum), just to reassure him that I was telling the truth.

We commenced foreplay on the couch, and he soon informed me that he wouldn't be kissing me with tongue because he had a canker sore on the inside of his mouth. "Stress," he said. It felt weird kissing just on the lips, but I soon convinced myself it was more simple and pure that way, like high school. Or junior high school. Another rule soon was established: I was not to bite him. "I just don't like it," he said. He then proceeded to pay a great deal of attention to getting my clothes off. His clothes remained for the most part intact, until finally he admitted he didn't like to take his shirt off in front of other people.

Forty-five minutes later I was naked and wriggling on two of his fingers, while he wore a T-shirt and boxers. We finally made a move to the bed, and then he whispered, "Do you want to have sex?"

"Yes," I said. I mean, of course I did. I always wanted to have sex. I wasn't quite sure what kind of sex I was going to have with him. I knew what kind of sex it wasn't going to be: sex with tongue, sex with biting, or sex with complete nudity—and, I was beginning to suspect, sex as equals. He wouldn't let me make him feel good. He just wanted to do things to me.

"Do you have a condom?" he said.

"I think so," I said.

"Well then before we do it, I have to ask you something," he said. "Have you been tested for sexually transmitted diseases?"

"Okay, what the fuck is going on here?" I said. I was pissed off—oh, that temper of mine—but also I was embarrassed. In that moment, for just a second, I felt like maybe he knew something I didn't know. That would be impossible, of course, but I couldn't figure out why he kept asking me the same question.

"I just need to know the answer to the question," he said.

"I have already answered you twice," I said.

"I have a right to ask these questions," he said. "I shouldn't feel uncomfortable for asking them."

"But I've already answered them."

"This is what will make me feel comfortable," he said. "If you answer the question."

I stood up and pulled on my pants and put on my bra. "I don't understand why you're treating me this way," I said. "This is complete bullshit."

"I shouldn't feel uncomfortable," he said. And then I noticed that his voice had changed. It had become almost robotic, and his long frame seemed to shrink into him. He was curling up in an emotional ball. "I have a right to ask these questions," he said again.

Something clicked in my head.

"Is this like someone washing their hands a lot?" I said. I couldn't think of the word for it.

He was silent. I grabbed my shirt and started to put it on.

"Yes," he said. "I have OCD." He had given up on medication years ago, and this was the way he had decided to live his life.

The constant questioning was a ritual he went through with every woman he dated, he explained. "It's a hurdle, but once you get over it, I promise you there's no other problems with sex," he said. "I like to have lots of sex."

I softened a bit. This was language I understood. Soon my pants were off, but again, it was about him doing things to me, him touching my breasts, him whispering dirty words in my ear, him stroking me all over. And I wanted to do the same to him, I wanted us both to get off. That's what turned me on: a mutual exchange. I reached my hand toward his shorts, and he shoved it away.

And that was it—that was the final blow. He had refused the gentle touch of my hand. I felt controlled, and not in a let's-play-some-sex-games sort of way. He was setting all the rules, and I knew one thing very clearly about myself: I was definitely not a rules girl.

"You can only see what you want," I told him. "It's all about you."

"I thought I was making you feel good," he said. "I thought we were having fun."

And we were, but of course, we weren't. I was confused. I couldn't be mad at him for being chemically imbalanced. He had been kind to me, and I knew he was capable of being a good partner to someone. I felt like he needed someone weaker than me, someone more willing to be dependent on someone, because he felt so weak himself.

We talked more that night, but eventually we passed out from exhaustion. In the morning he had to get up early (he was volunteering with the elderly, naturally, because he was just that nice of a guy), and when we said goodbye I got a little depressed. It was at that moment I realized I really was not a nice enough person to be with him. Someone could handle him, someone could work through everything, and in the end, they'd get a really good person. But not me.

Later on, when I found out that he'd had similar inter-actions with other women, that he had gone through years in his life where he'd had no sex at all, and that he'd also gone through periods of extreme sexual binges, that his sexuality was so wrapped up in his mental illness that there was no way I could have ever sustained a meaningful relationship with him, even after knowing all of that, in the end I still felt this small sting of regret, or maybe failure. I know you shouldn't personalize someone else's disease; it'll get you nowhere. Call it my own romantic OCD, but I still think about it all the time, I still want to ask him: why wouldn't you just fuck me?

Will Doig
THE MISSING PIECE

The only things that can lure me to the suburbs are sex and Dunkin' Donuts muffins. Dunkin' Donuts blueberry muffins come marbled with exquisite saturated fats like fine Kobe beef.

Sex is far less predictably appetizing, so when you're crossing the city line via surface transit for a questionable encounter with a stranger, you begin to wish you were heading muffinward instead. Nevertheless, this particular muggy June afternoon, I found myself on my way to the suburbs for the nonmuffin reason, from Washington, D.C., to the cultural abyss of Rockville, Maryland. I surveyed my fellow bus passengers. Most of them gazed despondently out their windows like freshly convicted inmates being transported to a facility for long-term supervision.

I was a vibrant twenty-year-old, and their despair inspired a smug twinge of superiority within me. Unlike them, I was being whisked toward adventure—and possible dismemberment—

after being persuaded by a man in an America Online M4M chat room to meet him "IRL." Because this was 1998, my 2,400-baud modem hadn't allowed me to download his photograph onto my Gateway 2000—all I knew was he was four years older than me and named Sean. I had written my own name on my bicep with a Sharpie in case my face was mutilated beyond recognition when they found my corpse suspended from a ceiling like in *Silence of the Lambs*.

The bus hissed to a halt across from a Blockbuster parking lot, and there was Sean, leaning on the hood of a sepia '81 Oldsmobile Delta like James Dean borrowing his grandpa's car. It was my favorite model of Oldsmobile, and the fact that he'd mentioned he owned one had played no small part in my decision to come out here, so I was relieved to find he was telling the truth. What's more, he was cute, with shaggy hair and a humanizing scorch of razor burn. He greeted me with a locked-elbow handshake while using his other hand to remove his sunglasses with a cartoonish Hollywood-agent sweep.

I was already eyeing the Dunkin' Donuts in the next parking lot over, but I knew Sean had made dinner reservations and I didn't want to be rude by buying a muffin for the ride to the restaurant.

"You like fish, right?" he said.

"Totally," I replied, thinking he meant the band. The massive hood of the car stretched out before us like a king-size bed as we soared down the interstate.

"I thought we could go to Legal Seafood," he said. "It's good."

"Good" if you live in a culinary tragedy like Rockville, I thought, but I smiled and nodded enthusiastically, immediately deciding to order the most expensive item on the menu.

I rolled down my huge passenger window and adjusted the side mirror so I could watch the car's exterior as we drove; the retreating sun set the chrome fenders ablaze. I felt wonderfully reckless, braver than anyone I knew. Who else would agree to meet a total stranger from the Internet? I was Indiana Jones stepping out over the chasm and onto the invisible bridge, a practitioner of modern-day derring-do.

Our waitress glowered at my driver's license, then snatched my wineglass and brusquely walked away. I sat there asexually, like a scolded child who'd just been caught cheating on a quiz. Sean ordered a glass of wine and I ordered a Sprite. He asked me some questions that were, if a bit bland, at least polite. I was used to lecherous guys who laced their questions with lewd innuendo, so the mild banality was refreshing.

In fact, everything about the blandness of this date—the corporate restaurant, the antiseptic shopping mall that housed the restaurant, Sean's nerdy demeanor—was strangely comforting. Living in the city, you almost don't realize how strenuous sociability is: the competitively witty banter, the desperately hip dating venues. I thought ahead to what Sean would be like in bed: quiet, orderly, very little foreplay.

Eventually, I remarked that because I was working for the local gay magazine in Washington, I would be manning a booth at next week's Gay Pride festival.

"So it's Gay Pride in D.C., huh?" he said with a snort, not looking up from his chowder.

"Yeah," I said. "Why? You want to go?"

"I don't think so."

"You should come. It's fun."

"Not my scene."

"C'mon."

"No." He was still staring into his dish, and his pitch had dropped half an octave lower into an unnatural baritone. We munched on our fish and hoped that the waitress would stop by to snap the awkward spell.

Then Sean said this:

"It just seems really weird to me that gay people go around asking for things like acceptance and tolerance and rights, and say stuff like, 'We're the same as straight people, so you shouldn't discriminate against us,' and then go and have parades in the middle of the city, and it's all pink floats carrying leather guys in chaps humping each other and flamey guys in rainbow Speedos simulating oral sex. I mean, gay people can't expect to ever be accepted into mainstream society if they do this stuff in public, and prance around like these screaming queens in front of families and kids and stuff."

"Right," I said automatically, trying to catch up. Had he referred to gay people as "they"? I suddenly had the bizarre idea that maybe this wasn't a date at all, but that Sean was straight and had simply been in the M4M chat room looking for a buddy to get some pan-roasted halibut with. Either way, this

debate wasn't something I wanted to dive into, so I phrased
a weak counterpoint designed to change the subject, which it
did, and the conversation resumed its tepid civility.

After dinner, we went back to his place, a small house
on a wooded street, where a large dog attacked me in the
kitchen with a continuous stream of deafening, bloodthirsty
barks. Sean made no move to restrain or soothe the animal,
but simply said, "That's Andy." Andy bared his fangs and
backed me into the refrigerator. A postcard from Italy jostled
loose and fluttered to the floor.

We ended up in Sean's living room watching TV. When
he turned it on, it was tuned to a channel called Fox News
that I'd vaguely heard of. He started to flip around. "Wait, go
back," I said. On the screen, Ken Starr was holding a press
conference. I'd been following the Monica Lewinsky story
like an addict. It was the most riveting thing that had ever
been broadcast. The last president to be impeached had been
Andrew Jackson for illegally ousting the secretary of war.
Now we got to watch our current president talk about blowjobs and improvised sex toys. It was excellent television.

"Ken Starr looks like a child molester," I said, settling
onto his couch. Sean harrumphed in reply.

"Hmm?" I said.

"No, nothing," he said. "I'm just amazed at people who
think Ken Starr is the bad guy in this. I mean, he's a prosecu-
tor. He's doing his *job*."

"Yeah, but is this really a good use of government resources?" I said. I wasn't particularly political at the time—to me, the Lewinsky thing was just a fun scandal—and it felt odd to be arguing a point about this.

"Don't you care if your president is immoral?" said Sean.

"No," I said. And I didn't. "They're all immoral, aren't they?"

"If he can lie to us about cheating on his wife, he's a liar and he should be impeached."

"I think that's crazy," I said, suddenly finding my political indignation. I'd never defended a politician. I'd voted for Clinton by reflex. But Sean's self-righteousness was too much. "Who the hell cares who sleeps with who?"

"Everyone!" he said loudly.

A momentary hush fell over the room. The only sound was Ken Starr grimly droning from a podium on the steps of a federal building. Sean and I were still sitting right next to each other on the couch, which suddenly felt too close.

"Are you a Republican?" I said.

"I'm registered Independent."

"But who did you vote for?"

"I voted for Dole," he said defiantly.

"Wow. So you're Log Cabin?"

"Can we not talk about this?" he said. The phone rang and Andy erupted into another Cujo-esque yowling spasm. Sean went to answer the phone, speaking quietly out in the kitchen.

When he came back, he was calmer. We immediately began making out on the couch so we wouldn't have to speak. There was nothing that could neutralize the awkwardness at this point except deranged Republican-on-Democrat sex. It had become clear to me that Sean had some serious self-loathing issues. I felt bad for him. I imagined him trolling the AOL chat rooms, trying to lure guys to Rockville because he couldn't bring himself to go near a gay bar.

Soon we were in his bedroom. It was one of those rooms where the roof is the ceiling, slanted at a thirty-degree angle. I saw his computer, a Dell, sitting on a desk on the side of the room where the ceiling was lowest. I realized that while Sean was sitting at the computer, he must have to hunch over so his face was nearly touching the monitor. It made the image of him whacking off with his free hand in a private chat room that much more depressing.

Our shirts came off. He was really, really skinny. Impossibly skinny. I could see his ribs through his chest hair. His pants came off. His kneecaps were roughly the size and shape of his hips. I'd never been with anyone with so little padding, and I was afraid I might hurt him if I tried to climb on top, so we squirmed side by side for a while like fish in a bucket. My arm was trapped under his torso and soon fell asleep.

"Your last name is Doo-ing?" he said, looking at my free arm.

"It's pronounced Doig, like foil or soil."

I moved my head toward his groin but he pulled me back up. I went for the nipple, but was again gently guided back to the kissing position. I decided I'd been wrong about the foreplay. I brought my hand up to his chest and felt nothing but rib cage. This was skinniness of a level that suggested impending death.

Oh my God.

"Do you have AIDS?" I said, holding my breath.

"Uh-uh."

"Uh-uh no?" I said.

"Definitely, positively not."

I relaxed a bit and sort of rubbed his bony chest cavity. It felt like I was running my hand across a picket fence.

That's when Sean said, "So I guess you've probably noticed I only have one pectoral muscle."

"What?"

"One pec," he said. He said it like he was saying, "So I guess you've probably noticed I reupholstered the couch."

"Does it gross you out?" he asked tentatively.

"Of course not," I said quickly, trying to make my sudden gag reflex sound like a cough.

"You sure?" he said. "Some guys are freaked out by it."

"Not me!" I said way too enthusiastically.

I moved back a bit and looked. One side of his chest was skinny, but normal. The other side was perfectly flat, the skin stretched tight, like it wasn't his skin but a suit of human skin that he was wearing. Like in *Silence of the Lambs*. Whoa.

"It's fine," I said. I felt awful for finding it repulsive, but I just wasn't ready for it. Had he told me in advance, and maybe let me take a peek before we were naked and on the verge of copulation, I might have dealt with it with more savoir-faire.

It dawned on me that this could very well be the reason Sean was a self-hating Republican who lived far from any sizable gay population—he'd probably received this very same reaction many times before, guys who rejected him because of his missing pec. Maybe some had even laughed at him for it. I felt a surge of sympathy. But sympathy is a hard-on killer. There was no way this was going to happen, so I said the words I'm sure he was dreading.

"How 'bout we just cuddle?"

He smiled like I'd just accidentally killed his dog with my car and he was trying to tell me it was okay. A smile-grimace. We settled into a spooning position, him behind me, his arm draped across my intact torso.

The next morning Sean dropped me at the Blockbuster parking lot. He didn't wait around for my bus to arrive. I watched his beautiful '81 Delta disappear down the street, as sturdy a car as they come. I didn't feel very brave or reckless. I felt shallow, another twenty-year-old who thinks his shit doesn't stink, who can't handle life's little imperfections without freaking out. The ride back to the city would feel like a retreat.

My bus wasn't due for another twenty minutes, so I walked into the Dunkin' Donuts in the next lot over and scanned the shelves.

"I'll have a blueberry muffin," I said to the cashier.

"Fresh out," she replied with a smile.

Pasha Malla

ALL ABOARD THE SHAME TRAIN

Some people are jet-setters. Some people wear fancy clothes with their hair up in that thing, thick with gel. Some people have shoes so pointy they could put your eye out with one errant kick. These are the Mile-High Club people, the people who make eyes at one another across the aisles of 747s and shuffle off to the toilets to do it, cramped and rocking about to the rhythm of atmospheric turbulence.

I am not one of these people. I am not in their Mile-High Club, nor do I ever anticipate being initiated. See, I take the train. My clothes, my hair, my shoes: all modest, all embarrassingly simple, nothing more angular or edgy than the rounded toes of my flip-flops.

But us train folks have a club of our own. In our club, there is no rush to the john to jostle around on the pee-splattered floor. No. We get one another's phone numbers and later rendezvous at a more hospitable location, a restaurant or a futon. Our club is a more patient brand: ground-bound, old-fashioned, but also dignified. Occasionally, though, it is sordid and guilt inducing.

I take the train a lot, and I've developed a system. I board last, sitting beside the prettiest girl I can find. I begin with small talk: "We are on the train. Let the jet-setters have their air miles and oxygen masks. You are pretty, and I may have weird protrusive ears and an excess of shoulder hair, but in essence we are the yin and yang of long-distance travel." Sometimes it works. I have gotten numbers from, and gone on dates with, train girls I normally would have no business even talking to.

When I was living in Toronto, one weekend I headed back to my hometown to visit my mom. I seated myself beside, and subsequently did my best to woo, the very friendly, Rachel McAdams—esque "Lisa," a student at the local School of Education. On our way to hail taxis, Lisa and I discovered that she and my mom lived in the same neighborhood, so we split a cab back to Lisa's place. The Choo-Choo Club, it seemed, was about to induct a new member.

At Lisa's, I was told to "hold on a sec" before she emerged from the basement with two long, stout snakes coiled around her arms. We spent the following half hour fully clothed and wordlessly transferring the snakes from her body to mine. They would slither down her wrists, onto my fingertips, and then wind themselves up to my shoulders before making their way back to Lisa. There was otherwise no touching, no kissing, nothing even vaguely sexual, but this was easily the most tantalizingly erotic—not to mention frighteningly bizarre—practice in which I had engaged with another human being.

Eventually Lisa put the snakes away and offered to drive me home. On the way, I asked her why she had been in Toronto, and Lisa said, "Visiting my mom," so I asked, "What does your mom do?" to which Lisa said, "She's in palliative care," so I said, "Oh," assuming that by this she meant that her mother worked in palliative care. Lisa dropped me off, we exchanged phone numbers and a quick kiss, and plans were made to do something the next evening.

The following evening, in typical Choo-Choo Club form: sex. Fortunately, the snakes remained locked up, but when we awoke the next morning, she had rug burn on her face and I had two black eyes and what I could only assume to be lockjaw. My body ached and there were bite marks up and down my arms. "I can't wait until we get *really* crazy," Lisa said, rolling on top of me and digging her fingernails into my scrotum.

From this, a routine developed. I had never met this type of woman, a woman who would morph from a dimpled, bashful schoolteacher-to-be into a rabid beast, foaming at the mouth and flinging the C-word around like an East Londoner out on a pub crawl. Otherwise, we talked very little. As I soon realized, it is almost impossible to have a conversation with a pillow pressed over your face.

One Friday night, I got a call from Lisa. She was in town. "Let's hook up," I said, feeling that familiar mix of arousal and fear that prefaced each rendezvous. "I can't," Lisa told me. Then, the bomb, dropping, exploding: "My mom just died."

I think I might have said something brilliant and sympathetic like, "Who?" or "How?" or possibly even both. Apparently Lisa's mom had been "in palliative care" for close to six months. "The funeral's tomorrow," said Lisa. "Do you have anything to wear?"

Have you seen the movie version of *High Fidelity*? Remember that part when the girl's dad or someone dies and all she wants to do is screw? Picture that, except think Linda Blair in *The Exorcist* meets the Tasmanian Devil meets Traci Lords after six years of solitary confinement. I know this sounds flippant and insensitive, but, honestly, at this stage Lisa was showing no signs of grief. My attempt at consolation—gentle murmuring with a hand rubbing circles on her back—was soundly rejected. That same hand was grabbed and stuffed between her legs, and my murmurs were stifled with a sock and duct tape.

Lisa came back to my place, claiming to be unable to face the outside world, to need a few days off. Fair enough. I called into work to explain that my "girlfriend's" mom had died. This was maybe a month after I had met Lisa on the train, and I'm sure Lisa had no pretenses that we were an official couple, either. Still, we were well beyond Choo-Choo Club now, and my function, I knew, had become strictly utilitarian. So I did my best to comply.

One evening, about three days into our sessions of sex therapy, there was a power surge (I blame the amount of electrical gadgets Lisa had plugged into the power bar in my bedroom) and the lights went out. This happened just as we were finishing. I had taken a sound haymaker to the chin, and then: boom. Darkness. I scrambled around naked until I found a flashlight and illuminated Lisa, who was sitting on the bed gazing at me, that familiar, heavy-lidded look in her eyes. "Hey," she said. "Come here." I stood fast. "Come on. Bring the flashlight." I wavered. "Now."

As I sat down, Lisa took the flashlight from my hand. "Bend over," she said. "I'm going to fuck you with this." My first thought, oddly enough, was whether she was planning on leaving it on, and I pictured my rectum lit up like a cave. I tried to imagine my mom dying and how that would feel, but instead I could only think about how the flashlight would feel. I surmised it would be like trying to swallow a bus. I looked at Lisa, a golden beam of light streaming from her hand. That thing? In my bum?

I couldn't do it. My sympathy only extended so far. So I lied, made up something about hemorrhoids, diarrhea, I forget, and then flopped over onto my back and lay tightly against the sheets. I held my arms out. "Hug?" I offered. Lisa snorted, clicked the flashlight off, then went downstairs to sleep on the couch.

The next day, without ceremony, Lisa left, abandoning me with my own guilt. Would it have been so bad? I mean, a few minutes of pain versus her lifetime of grief—it hardly seemed a fair comparison. Still, I took comfort in knowing there had to be someone out there with a bigger heart and a more welcoming backside than mine.

Shortly thereafter, I took an extended leave from my job and found a cheap ticket to Paris. The limits of the Choo-Choo Club tested, it seemed time to try a little jet-setting of my own. High above the Atlantic Ocean, after a few sideways glances, I made eye contact with a young woman across the aisle. She nodded her head in the direction of the rear cabin, the toilets.

I wish I could tell you that I went back there and became the member of that other, more prestigious club, ravaged some stranger with her legs up on the sink, pointy shoes to the heavens. I wish I could claim that afterward we emerged disheveled and sated, and returned to our seats without exchanging a word. And, while we're at it, I wish I could tell you that my flight to Paris was not made out of fear—fear, my friends, and also shame. I wish I could tell you all these things. I really, really, really wish I could.

Scott Mebus

WORKING RELATIONSHIP

I met Kira right about the time my job crossed the line from barely palatable to fantastically dull. My altruistic superiors had decided that I would do my work best in my own office. This would have been happy news if not for the fact that the only available office lay clear on the other side of the floor. So off they packed me, exiled to the south side, an elevator bank and two security card swipes away from my fellow coworkers. Gazing about my windowless closet, I realized how easily I could slip into a *Shining*-esque insane murderous rage if left to my own devices. So I was thinking of the lives of the people around me when I forsook my work to wander the halls in search of human interaction.

It was during my wanderings that I stumbled upon Kira. Tucked away in a forgotten corner, her tiny office rivaled mine in both size and solitude. Her boss worked in another building altogether, leaving her to slowly waste away in her little, lost cubbyhole. So there really was no getting around it. She could have been a snake-worshiper or a fifth-level dungeon master; our friendship was inevitable.

At first glance she appeared to be neither of these things, nor any of the other thousand deviant personalities that leapt to mind. A blend of Asian and Polish, Kira's features tilted toward the exotic, but an everyday, approachable exotic. Sort of a vaguely Asian Kelly Clarkson, the multicultural girl-next-door. She seemed nice enough, and I'll admit on first meeting her my mind ran through some preliminary scenarios for my penis's approval. But she lacked something. Maybe it was a pheromone thing, or maybe it was her Hello Kitty backpack. Something about her didn't flick my tuning fork.

This didn't stop us from flirting, of course. She could have been the mom from *What's Eating Gilbert Grape*, and I'd still flirt. Nothing major, of course. Just some light mockery with a dash of inside humor. Your typical office stuff, on my end anyway. Kira had her own style, her personal twist to the game. It was . . . interesting.

I first noticed her method after a week or so. She'd added an Ash, from *Army of Darkness*, action figure to her array of knickknacks. I had to congratulate her on her good taste in cult films.

"Nice Ash."

She raised an eyebrow.

"Are you mocking the greatest film of all time? Or making an inappropriate pun?"

"No," I protested. "I just love your Ash. It rocks."

"You are so rude! Get out!"

I laughed, deciding to move past the joke.

"So where did you get him? A gift?"

"I'm not kidding. Get out of my office."

I hesitated. Her mouth curved upward in a smirk, betraying her playful mood. But she sounded serious.

"I . . . I was talking about the action figure," I said finally, trying to end the game.

"I'm not talking to you anymore."

With that, she pushed me out of her office and shut the door in my face.

I didn't know what to make of this extreme reaction. I stopped by after lunch to demand some answers, but Kira glossed over the whole episode. In fact, she seemed even more comfortable with me than before my remark. I soon learned that taking offense was her main flirtation device. If I went just a little too far, out would come the shocked expression, the exclamation of disapproval, and the inevitable "I'm not talking to you anymore." Eventually, I got used to it. Maybe she was just a remedial flirter and this was her odd attempt at pulling my pigtails. I wasn't about to push away my only cohort on the south side, so I learned to live with her eccentricities.

Then the Red Sox came to town.

It was a beautiful summer night in the Bronx. Kira had scored company seats and invited me along. As huge Yankee fans, we couldn't wait to see our hometown boys beat the living crap out of those Boston wife-beaters (a rumor I'm starting). We lost twelve to two. That isn't an excuse for what followed, merely an explanation. I was at a low point in my life. Times were hard. Mistakes were made. There should be free passes for sex perpetrated under certain horrible circumstances. Funerals. Wars. Terminal diseases. Losing by double digits to the Red Sox. I was in mourning and I reached out for comfort.

We've all done it. Crossed the line we swore we'd never cross. Made the move we swore we'd never make. And hey, a small, eternally optimistic voice inside invariably pipes up with the chipper thought that maybe this will work out. Maybe we'll *When Harry Met Sally* this bad decision into a long and happy marriage. Hell, there is no more accomplished dream-weaver than the owner of an erect penis. Which is how Kira and I ended up mauling each other on my ratty old couch.

I first noticed a problem after we'd been kissing awhile. Sure, Kira and I had a weird flirt pattern, but I wasn't worried about it. Once the lovin' starts, we all regress to the mean. After all, the flirtation objective has been reached. Once the hands begin to roam, all previous attitudes take a backseat to the almighty passion, the great equalizer, as predictable as the regret. Some might pull out handcuffs while others reach for their special dildo briefcase, but our passion is one accessory we always provide. I guess you'd call it booty etiquette. As a rule, people don't begin talking dirty in a Howard Cosell voice, or dryly calculate aloud the equation for the correct velocity needed to generate a clitoral orgasm. We breathe heavy, sweat copiously, and generally make an effort. It's only polite. But with Kira, somehow we veered away from Miss Manners. It started with a compliment.

"I love your breasts. They're perfect on you."

She leaned back to stare at me with furrowed brow.

"What do you mean they're perfect on me?"

"I mean they're the perfect size for your body."

She covered the objects of conversation with her arm, her lips curling upward in the faintest hint of a smirk.

"So on someone else's body they'd be freakish?"

"No, not at all. I mean you look great."

"As long as my body doesn't change, which would leave me with the wrong size breasts."

"I'm trying to give you a compliment!"

"I'm not talking to you anymore."

Nothing had changed. You'd think we were arguing over her stupid action figure again instead of halfway through some serious pants removal. Did she think she still needed to flirt? My hand was up her shirt: mission accomplished. It got worse once we lost the clothes and made it to my bed. I buried my head between her legs, diving into my patented specialty. After a moment, I brought forth the fingers, moving into stage two of Operation: Oral. That's when she grabbed my hair.

"Hey! Who said you could stick those in there!"

I pulled my fingers back.

"I'm trying to get you ready."

She crossed her arms again.

"Then keep licking, cowboy. You have to lick till I say I'm ready for the fingers. Didn't your mother teach you anything?"

Not about this, thank God.

"Maybe we should just move to stage three," I said, starting to rise toward her. She put a hand on my head and pushed back.

"No! You are not gypping me out of my lick-time!"

Looking up, I could swear she was smirking at me. Like this was a game. Okay, fine. Determined to beat her, I proceeded to lick away.

"Not so fast," she said. "I'm not a water bowl, Lassie."

Fed up but refusing to give in, I replied with my middle finger, while licking even faster. She snorted.

"Hey, at least you're keeping it where I can see it."

Was that a challenge? I knew how to answer that one.

"Whoa!" she said, wriggling. "That finger is definitely not supposed to go there."

I ignored her.

"Hey, stop it right there!" she said. "You reach a knuckle, you are toast, mister."

But she didn't pull away. She simply stared at me, smirking, *daring* me.

I leaned back and yanked on a condom so hard I almost burst through it. She raised her eyebrows.

"Didn't have the jaw for the job, huh?"

Now, I'm not normally a competitive person. But right then, all I wanted was to shut her up. And the only way I knew I could make that happen would be to drag her by the ear toward such an earth-shattering orgasm that she wouldn't have the breath to annoy me anymore. Thrusting inside her, I began to pace myself, finding that zone where marathon runners and priests hearing confession lived. The place where I could go forever. But that's when I noticed her smirking again.

"So it's gonna be that way, huh?" she said.

I guess I wasn't the only one in it to win it. She began doing some strange breathing technique while moving her hips. A crack appeared in my calm. She bit her lower lip seductively. Another crack. And then she pulled out the kegel muscles.

"No fair!" I cried.

"All's fair," she replied.

So that's the way she wanted to play it. I settled in for the long haul. After half an hour, we were still at it, going strong. That's when the trash talking started up.

"You okay?" she asked, eyes flashing. "You look beat. Sure you wouldn't rather just pop your cork and catch the rest of *South Park*?"

"I'm doing great. You?"

"I could go all night."

"Great. Me too."

"Great."

"You sure you're not starting to feel it? How about that?" I gave her a double thrust. "You know you're close. You sound like you're gonna . . ."

"You worry about yourself, big shot. Don't think I can't hear you breathing heavy."

"That's because it's been, like, two hours. I need a water break."

"Well all you have to do is come, and you'll get your water."

"You first, darling. You first."

"HEY!" she cried as I made my move. "No manual assistance. Get your finger off my clit!"

"I thought all's fair?" I answered, giving her a two-finger flick. "Do you like that?"

She blinked innocently.

"I'm sorry, were you doing something? I was miles away."

"You are the devil."

This might sound like fun. But it wasn't fun. There's nothing enjoyable about screwing long after the need to screw has been stomped to death. It became a war of attrition, a battle of wills—until finally, my will gave out.

"That's disappointing," she said, staring at my dick lying limp in the dry condom.

"If I can't win, nobody wins," I said, penis aching, nerves stretched to the snapping point. All I wanted to do was throw her out the window and go to sleep.

"Well, at least we had fun playing!" she said, stretching languorously. She sighed a happy sigh and turned to snuggle.

I started looking for a new job the very next day. Some signs you just can't ignore.

Shalom Auslander

TROUBLE IN PORNOLAND

Early signs for sex that evening were positive: it was not yet eight o'clock, the baby was asleep, and neither my wife nor I had been overly exhausted by another difficult day on this too-trying Earth, nor overly depressed, nor overly angry, nor overly murderous, nor overly suicidal. As my wife showered, I sat with my laptop on our bed, responding to some late e-mails and sipping a glass of wine. It is a fact that the probability of any evening's marital sexual relations is directly proportional to the length of either partner's shower that said evening, and she had been in there for some time now. When she finally emerged from the bathroom, wrapped in a towel and chased by a gentle billow of steam, I was pleased to see her head straight for her lingerie drawer.

"Hey," I said, "you're not the regular poolboy."

"Just thought I'd come by, ma'am," she said, "see if anything was too *wet*."

I laughed, and then she laughed, and as she turned and headed back into the bathroom, she asked if we had any decent porno we could watch.

"No," I said, "but we have broadband."

"Even better," she said, closing the door behind her.

It's important for you to know at this point that me and porno go way back. Me and porno are buddies. Me and porno, we hang.

When I was a nine-year-old Orthodox yeshiva student, I found a pile of discarded pornography magazines in the woods behind my house. Compared to the physical world around me—a world of overwhelming religious restriction and suffocating social regulations—the fantasy world of pornography seemed like a parallel (if gooey) version of the Garden of Eden my rabbis had just described to me; legs were eternally spread, bodies were proudly exposed, heads were thrown back in ecstasy. In porno there was no guilt, no shame, no fear, no anger. Black people fucked white people, white people fucked black people, men fucked women, women fucked women, and, in a magazine named *Blueboy*, buried at the very bottom of the pile, men even fucked men. People in Pornoland ate pussy, they ate ass, they ate come. Was come kosher, I wondered? Was there a blessing on pussy? The people of Pornoland didn't seem to care, and I loved them for it. With inspiring abandon, women lavished attention and in turn were lavished upon, and men spilled their seed on the floor and the chair and the couch and the bellies and the backs and the faces and the lips without fear of retribution, without worry about damnation and without concern for the purgatorial postdeath punishment one rabbi had described to us that year; of being boiled alive for eternity in a vat of all the semen you wasted during your lifetime. Licking, sucking, pinching, fucking: do what you want, the leaders of Pornoland declared, but judge not, scorn not, worry not. Paradise. Perhaps this had been Walt Disney's idea when he created Disneyland—a place, first and foremost, free of anger. But Mickey didn't have a cock, and Minnie didn't have a pussy, and so I wasn't all that impressed with their idyllic existence. John Holmes, though. Ginger Lynn. Wendy Whoppers. Now there was a group I could emulate. I admired their daring, their rebellion, their freedom. They made me feel better about myself, as rabbis both dead and alive did everything they could to make me feel the opposite. So I was surprised when, a few years later, I saw people—*nonreligious people!*—in Manhattan—*Manhattan!*—protesting pornography. *Pornography!* I had recently begun yeshiva high school on 181st Street, and had cut Talmud class to go to Times Square. It wasn't long before my backpack was filled with hardcore magazines and videocassettes, and I was a couple blocks away from the bus stop on 47th and 5th when I passed an angry woman shouting into a megaphone and waving a wooden placard above her head. On the placard was a large still-frame from a hardcore porno movie: a large-breasted blonde woman on her knees, eyes closed, getting done from behind by an ecstatic black man. I was about to ask her where I could find such a movie when I noticed her friend carrying another placard that read "Porn = Hate!"

Really? I wondered. I thought it =ed "liberty." I thought it =ed "escape." I thought it =ed "fun."

Lunatic, I thought to myself.

And where the *hell* did she get that movie?

The door to the bathroom opened again, and my wife climbed into bed beside me. We sat side by side, the laptop between us, and underneath the "Bookmarks" heading in the Web browser, I selected an online porno forum I used to frequent. It had been a while since I'd been to that site, though—the combination of a pregnancy, a newborn baby, and the stress of raising an infant hadn't ruined our sex life as completely as some had predicted, but it had made pornography somewhat inconvenient—when you have barely the time or the energy for the main feature, so to speak, who can be bothered with the previews? I clicked on the first forum entry, and screen caps of the downloadable videos began to appear.

"Jesus Christ," said my wife once the page had loaded.

Now listen, I have had bad days before. I have been fired from jobs, I have been dumped by girlfriends, I have totaled cars. I have had days where I have received three—count 'em, three—tickets for speeding or moving violations between nine A.M. and nine P.M. But I have never had a day as bad as a woman named "Cloey" had the day they shot the video that appeared on that page—that is to say, I have never had a day where someone wrote the word "cockwhore" on my forehead with lipstick, tried to shove their entire fist down my throat, and then "choke-fucked" me with their penis until I barfed on their testicles. Never, ever had a day like that. Nor have I ever had a day like the blonde woman in the movie pictured below Cloey: I never had a day where someone hung a toilet seat around my neck, spit in my mouth, and slapped my face as he tried to shove the head of his cock through the back of my skull.

Bad days I have had. But not that bad.

"Jesus. Fucking. Christ," said my wife.

We sat like that, side by side, proclaiming disbelief as I scrolled farther down the page, the subject headings for the forum entries sounding like the police blotter from a place Snake Plissken might have escaped:

GIRL SLAPPED!

CHICK STUFFING BASEBALL BATS INTO HER CUNT!

HARD ANAL, THROATFUCKING, AND PUKING (A LOT!)

PERFECT SLUT EXTREMELY HARD TREATED— MUST SEE!

This was the description of that last one the poster had included with his screen caps:

"This scene has everything: blowjob, gagging, ass-to-mouth, rimming, assfuck, streched holes—there is nothing left!"

"Nice work, man!" another poster responded to the original poster.

"Thanks a lot for all these fine videos," responds another.

"Very, very good post," from a third. "Thanks a lot for sharing."

Such politeness, given the nature of the video, is only funny if it isn't your stretched holes they happen to be discussing.

This was not some "extreme sex" forum. That forum existed at the bottom of the page—"Paid Members ONLY"— though I can't imagine what sort of headings might be found there.

No, this was the regular forum. This was the main-stream. This was porn, 2007.

I know I'm supposed to be okay with this. I know I shouldn't judge. I know that I'm showing my age or my prud-ishness or my conservatism or my narrow-mindedness. But I'm thinking about those porn protesters back on the corner of 46th and 6th, sometime in 1985, and I'm beginning to wonder if porno in 2007 isn't proving them right; it's diffi-cult to present a credible defense against charges of hatred and misogyny when the star witness has the word "cunt" written on her forehead and a guy named Max Hardcore is urinating in her mouth. A moment with my client, Your Honor.

My wife sat back and pulled the covers over her legs.

"Do guys really want that?" she asked.

"Looks that way," I said.

It didn't look that way because of one forum. It looked that way because the *Gag Factor* series of films, in which women are turned upside down and choke-fucked until their faces are covered with drool, semen, and barf (Adult Video News Award Winner, "Best Oral Series,") is now up to sequel #22. Because the *Slap Happy* series, in which a male performer pauses from asphyxiating the starlet with his penis only to slap her repeatedly across the face and verbally abuse her, is up to sequel #13.

What happened to my wonderful porno?

What happened to that oasis of playful, heathenish fornication?

What happened to my cheesy pool boy?

I'm afraid he's "punch-fucking" some girl's ass while calling her a dirtywhorecuntslut. And I think I'm right.

My wife pulled on her robe, and I blew out the candle she had lit on the nightstand.

Ginger Lynn had made me feel free.

The Devil in Miss Jones made me feel better about my own devils.

But *Meatholes (Nasty whores who love to be treated like worthless pieces of meat!)* makes me feel exactly the way my rabbis wanted me to feel—makes me feel just as self-loathing and disgusted with sex as a community full of ultra-Orthodox lunatics were convinced I should be. So who's the worthless piece of meat now?

My wife went into the kitchen, made some tea, and grabbed some biscuits while I went to YouTube and found an episode of *South Park*.

We watched and laughed and sipped our tea and soon my wife asked, "Do you think these kids will want to do that to women when they get older?"

"I think Stan will be gay," I said. "And I think Cartman already wants to."

We finished our biscuits, shut down the computer, and went to sleep. I wonder how I'm going to explain all this to my son. I wonder what happened to the people in Pornoland. And I wonder how many of you only read this far in the hopes of finding out the name of that Web site.

Arthur Bradford

GROUPIE

This was in Austin, Texas, about seven years ago, the night when the all-women Swedish heavy-metal band came to town. Some friends of mine had been hired as their opening act, and I went along to check out the show. The Swedish women didn't get on stage until about one A.M. and the place had pretty much emptied out. But the band was incredible. They really knew how to rock. Their music was very loud and they stomped around the stage in high platform boots, shaking their wild metal hair like banshees. They even had a set of high-powered fans to keep their long locks flying in the wind. It was quite a thrill to watch. Because of my association with the opening act, I was able to view the show from backstage.

Unfortunately, the band only got about three or four songs into their set before a tussle broke out in the crowd. In some ways, this made sense, because the sight of these women rocking out was more than most of us guys could

take. It unleashed the kind of aggression you often see late
at night in male-dominated bars. It was pretty standard
for a Texas metal show, but during the melee someone set off
a canister of pepper spray. This got sucked into those wind
machines, and suddenly everyone around the stage went
blind and started to cough. I inhaled a lungful of the stuff
and nearly barfed.

I stumbled for the side door and opened it up. I was
about to leave the building when I saw that no one was helping the band. One of the guitarists was rubbing her eyes and
seemed like she might fall off the stage. So I went over there
and helped her out the door. The drummer and singer joined us
in the fresh air, and when we caught our breath, they thanked
me in their sexy Swedish accents.

"You are very nice to do that," said the guitar player.

"It was no problem," I said.

I felt like a real hero. We drank some beer while the cops
cleared the place out and handcuffed somebody for causing the
stir. The Swedes seemed to be under the impression that I was
in the band that had opened for them, which was okay by me
since it gave me a little more legitimacy in their eyes. I imagined they got approached by a lot of male fans while on tour.
We talked about life on the road and the rock-and-roll lifestyle,
and then it was time for them to go back onstage. The singer
was pretty mad about the whole thing and kept taunting the
crowd and giving them the finger. The club had really thinned
out at this point, and the show was sort of a bust. A couple of

times I noticed that the guitarist looked over at me and smiled and this kind of gave me goose bumps.

When the show ended, I hung around and tried to catch her eye, but the band went off into some backroom without talking to anybody. I figured my chance at heavy-metal love was lost. I left the club and joined my friends at another nearby bar. After a few drinks I was filled with newfound courage and made my way back to the club. A big tour bus was parked out front. What a great life, I thought, four Swedish babes rocking across America.

The door to the bus opened. It was the singer, still angry about the broken-up show. She saw me and said, "Oh, it's you."

Then she stuck her head back in the bus and said, "Eva, your friend is here."

I was about to correct her and say I wasn't really her friend, that we'd just met, but then Eva showed up, slightly tipsy, holding a lit cigar. She said, "Come on in."

I followed her up into the tour bus, a darkened smoke-filled chamber crowded with black-clad rock-and-rollers. We went to the back, where a small group was drinking aquavit, a very strong Swedish liquor. I had a few sips and felt dizzy. Eva sat next to me but almost immediately began talking to another man, in Swedish. I felt pretty out of place.

Slowly the bus began to clear out, and Eva turned her attention to me. I don't remember what we discussed, but I think I asked her about Sweden and she said Americans were dumb, or funny, something like that. At some point she figured out that I wasn't a musician, that I was just a fan, but at that point this didn't seem to bother her. Then the bus engine started, and I sat up.

"We're moving," I said.

"Yes," she said. "It's time to go."

"Okay," I said, getting up to leave.

"No, no," she laughed. "You will stay here."

"Stay here?"

"You come with us."

We'd been talking for about ten minutes, and I wasn't even sure where this bus was going, but it seemed like a fine idea to me. Eva had been so confident in her invitation, as if it was understood I would say yes. I felt flattered, really, that she had chosen me to stay. I sat back on the plush cushion, very satisfied with myself. I was on a tour bus with an all-women Swedish heavy-metal band. Excellent.

I thought perhaps we were headed somewhere in town, another club, or possibly a hotel, but the bus turned onto the highway and I realized then that we were traveling to the next town, wherever that was.

Shortly after we hit the highway, the various band members got into their bunks and closed the curtains. The drummer and her boyfriend, another Swede, took the big bed in the back. Eva and I sat on a couch up front and made out for a while. She was an aggressive, wet kisser, and her mouth tasted a bit like a cigar, but I enjoyed this moment very much. Eventually, though, something about the motion of the bus, the cigar taste, the aquavit, and the big bus driver sitting three feet away made me queasy.

Eva offered to share her bunk with me, so we clambered up there into this little compartment. I was hoping we could continue our make-out session up there, but things were pretty cramped and not conducive to romance. I tried to sleep, but it felt like there was something sticking in my back. Later I realized it was her guitar. She slept with it in her bunk. After a while, I moved onto the couch up by the driver and fell asleep there. As I drifted off, I remember thinking, "This is so cool. I am now dating a guitarist for a Swedish metal band." I had nifty thoughts about our future, how I might join them on a tour of Europe, or at least how she would call me up when they were in town again.

I woke up in bright sunshine at a gas station in west Texas. Everyone was hungover and in a foul mood. Eva didn't even want to get out of bed. I went to a diner with the drummer and her boyfriend and we ate steak and eggs, which tasted very good. The boyfriend didn't speak English so well. The night before, I had thought he was Swedish, but now I thought maybe he was German and it wasn't clear if he was even her boyfriend. Anyway, they both seemed to feel sorry for me. I was trying to figure out what town we were in, or at least what direction we'd been driving. Eventually I learned we were near El Paso.

The band had to do a promotional event at a record store in town that afternoon. Eva, who had looked so stunning and friendly just a few hours ago, now seemed sort of scary. I was afraid to talk to her, afraid she might not know who I was. But before she went into the record store she walked by me and pinched my ass. I was very happy that she did that. I spent the rest of the day with Rutger, the drummer's boyfriend. We got drunk in a bar. Although our conversations were limited by his halting English, he did say one thing that stuck in my head. He called me a "groupie."

It may seem strange that I was surprised to be called a groupie at that point, but the truth was I hadn't thought of myself like that. I thought groupies were scantily clad women who gave blowjobs backstage. Somehow this situation seemed different to me because I was a man. Most women, after all, could pick up strange men without having to be in a band. I thought I had won Eva's heart by saving her from the pepper spray and then charming her on the bus. But then I looked at Rutger and the crew of other desperate scraggly young men hanging around, and I realized I was no different. We were just like those girls you see up front at rock shows in tight clothing, proudly displaying their hard-earned backstage passes. Even if we weren't getting laid, we were happy just to be "with the band."

That night I went to the show and watched from backstage. The band was great again. The front row was packed with wide-eyed guys hooting and hollering. I had gotten over my groupie realization and felt very proud to be associated with this band in any way I could. After the show they had to sign some CDs and talk to someone from their record company. Rutger went to sleep on the bus, but I didn't feel qualified to do that. Instead, I hung around like a loser, waiting for some kind of attention from the band. I was even happy when the roadies acknowledged me.

When I finally saw Eva, she once again pinched my ass, and once again I was happy. But then I saw her do the same thing to another guy, and I wondered if perhaps I should just leave. I stuck it out, though, having no better options, and eventually made it onto the bus, where I was able to talk to Eva for about five minutes. I gave her my phone number, and she asked if I wanted to keep going with them to Phoenix, but I wasn't sure if she really wanted me to, or what that meant. I still had this fantasy that we'd start dating, and I figured the best move at this point was to play it cool and act like I had things to get back to in Austin.

So I got off the bus and went to the Greyhound station, where I slept on a bench until six A.M., when the next bus to Austin left town. I made it home in a daze, and for the next few days my heart jumped whenever the phone rang. But Eva never did call me up. When I told the story to my friends, I thought they would think I was very cool. But most of them said, "You're a groupie." One friend even suggested that Eva had used me.

But I didn't see it like that. Even though she'd pinched my ass and forgotten my name before the band reached Phoenix, I didn't feel used by Eva. In a sense, there was a simple sweetness to the way all of us followed those rock-and-roll women around. We wanted them to need us for something, and maybe they did, even if it wasn't sex, as we had hoped. I wonder if those girls who followed Mötley Crüe in the '80s didn't feel the same sense of noble purpose, like they had somehow helped the band rock America.

About a year after that show in Austin, I saw that the Swedish band was playing at Ozzfest down in San Antonio. Although I hadn't heard from Eva since we parted ways, I still got a ticket and went down there. There they were, tearing it up on the side stage, looking great, with a bunch of young metalheads shaking their fists to the beat. I went around back to the V.I.P. gate and was met by a large security guard.

"I'm friends with the band," I said.

"Sure you are," he said, shaking his head.

"No really," I said, my voice trailing off, "I am . . ."

Lisa Carver

DRUNK AND DISORDERLY

Sex with drunks, in general, is not good sex. When you're with drunks, you drink like they do, and it's just *so much sugar*—I think that's what inspires the physical activities you haven't engaged in since middle school, like finding out how many cartwheels you can do in a row. After that, you're tired. By the time you finally make it to bed, you're satisfied just to be able to accomplish the act at all.

That's with a normal drunk. Jerry was special.

I remember the first time Jerry and I didn't do it. We were in Jenny Mae's bed, and he suddenly realized it was her "marriage bed," and he stopped me. "I need sex to be spiritual, not animalistic," he said, and I thought he was joking, or high. He *was* high, with the deadly seriousness that only the coked out can achieve . . . an apex of lugubriousness. I found it alluring. I stared at the gauziness of Jenny Mae's draping canopy, the mysterious bloodstain right next to the butterfly, while Jerry spun a gauzy argument out of Dostoyevsky and Wolfe and Hume quotes.

I remember the second time we didn't do it, lying in Jerry's single bed with our injuries from the day pulsing (sliding into bases at softball, and falling off a wall), and the phone ringing, and his cat box and cigarettes combining fumes. He told me he was going to get his pilot's license and take me away from all this. I held his hand in the dark in the space between us on the bed and I believed him.

The times we did do it, he was cock-blocking. Or vagina-blocking, as I swung any which way back then. You would have too, if you were Jerry's semigirlfriend. He would have sex with me only to keep me from having sex. Because he loved me. And because he was a nut. He'd also go to AA meetings to try to take up the last seat and save someone from actually trying to get sober. He didn't believe in getting sober any more than he believed in getting lucky. On a visit to New York, he saved me from the twin threat of a Latin banshee and a dominatrix. He dragged me out from under them back to our hotel room, put his cigarette out on the white wall, and said, "Are you going to allow yourself to be controlled by beauty?" I thought, "Hm. Maybe." And then he did to me, all across the bed, carpet, and right up that cigarette-burned wall, everything that the banshee and the dominatrix would have, had they been allowed to have their citified lesbianistic way.

Despite our sloppiness, sex with Jerry felt precious, like a very old home movie that might break forever at any second.

It had the taste of sadness to it, and a terrible, unexplained urgency. I know this is a teenagery thing to say, but it was suicide sex, every time.

Courtly love formed out of the eleventh century's idea that people shouldn't do it, even when they're married. But, you know, even in the eleventh century, people had feelings, they had urges. So a knight would write passionate, explicit poetry to a married lady up in a castle and she would give him her scarf, which he would tie onto his lance (heh heh) and take all that sexual frustration into battle with him and do well at jousting, and that was honor. Honor was a big deal then.

Honor was not a big deal to anyone I'd met so far in the twenty-first century, except for Jerry, who would sit at Larry's bar for *hours,* writing maybe ten words on a peeled-off label, thinking about honor. That was how we met: him protecting me from sex by having sex with me. It was backstage with Nashville Pussy, with whom he was touring. He mistook me for a Nashville Pussy groupie, and he said I was too innocent. No one had ever described me as innocent before. I found it so surprising, I neglected to explain I was actually there as a journalist, to do an interview. And so right there and then, on that ripped and ratty backstage couch, bravely did he shield my body from Nashville Pussy with his own.

Another of the rare times I managed to have my way with that wayward man, it was because I choked on my vitamin pill at a café. His band mate Falcon swooped like his namesake onto that slimy pill and popped it in his own mouth. In that proxy saliva exchange, Jerry could see the writing on the wall. To protect me from Falcon's next maneuver, Jerry took me to the bathroom himself.

How was that sex in the café bathroom, which I'd been waiting for so long and with such longing? Kind of bad. But sincere. Like a middle-aged guidance counselor awkwardly dancing with a wallflower at a sixth-grade dance, when he's never danced before, but he's doing it with loving pity and it's really very sweet, though you don't appreciate that at the time, and everyone watching thinks it's creepy.

And people DID find Jerry creepy.

"You fucked Jerry Wick?" exclaimed Jenny Mae when she found out. "Nobody fucks Jerry Wick. I've never met one girl who would fuck Jerry Wick. Everybody hates him in Ohio. His ass has been kicked by about everybody. He's pissed off more people. . . . Always yelling about Cuba or the *Hindenburg,* things that happened long ago that no one cares about."

Jerry loved all things that no one cares about. He hated exploitive dramas about rape and pedophilia like *CSI.* He loved *Clueless* and *Days of Our Lives.* In those shows, no one got hurt sexually, lives did not shatter, and when the kissing began, Vaseline got spread over the camera lens to make it misty, to be followed by a gentle fade-out.

When Jerry heard I was getting married, he called and told me not to do it. I said, "Why not?" He said, "Because the guy you're about to marry doesn't understand you." I said, "How do you know that?" He said, "Because anyone who

really knew you would know you're not the marrying kind."
He was right, but I didn't want him to be, so I felt insulted and
said, "How do *you* know what kind I am?" He said, "You have
the worst reputation I've ever heard of. Let's not live up to it.
Our reputation. Let's go rent a little house down South, have
an apple tree."

What did that guy know about down South? What did
he know about apple trees? He couldn't even take four days in
a row of me on visits, and now he's talking about snatching me
from the altar and keeping me? He could only handle the idea
because it was all symbols. In the same way every word was a
symbol at Larry's, in the cool dark, hiding from the afternoon.
Everything in Jerry was shifting, illusory, full of possibility.
Nothing you could hold on to or count on. I fantasized about
going back to him, but I knew I never would. Other seedy
people out there needed him to mistake them for innocent, and
so become so, for just a moment.

David Amsden

THE INCOMPLETE TRIANGLE

She wanted one more drink before going home. Knowing I was already drunk, and the sort of things she was capable of when drunk, I knew this was a terrible idea. But I was twenty then, and terrible ideas always seemed like the ones that made the most sense, and so I tightened my hand around her waist, grinned, and said that sounded like a brilliant plan. Besides, that girl . . . what can I tell you? I wanted to eat her long red hair. I wanted to eat the soap she used. I was a mess. She lived on my block, and I'd spent a year watching her from afar—her pale dancer's body in those clothes that concealed nothing, that vacant smirk on her face, her presence at once inviting and impossible—and now that I was finally with her it felt even more unreal. "Let's get one more," she said, but she could have said, "Hey, before we go home why don't I stick razors under your fingernails," and I would've said yes, sure, please, anything. I'm exaggerating, of course. But not much.

She added, "Let's go to Henrietta Hudson's."

Which meant the lesbian bar around the corner from my apartment, a kind of nadir (so the magazines said) of West Village lesbianism. This was new. This changed everything. That Stephanie was into girls was something I should have already known. "I'm into girls, too," she'd told me once while drinking red wine from the bottle on my rooftop. "Just in case that freaks you out." But the thing about such statements is that, to a straight man, they mean nothing. The male ego, so narrow and fragile, doesn't respond well to matters that have nothing to do with us directly, especially when such matters involve sexual acts we're not physically equipped for. And so when a girl tells you she's into girls it's vaguely tantalizing, sure, but it remains murky, abstract, a college girl's endearing attempt at edginess. But when the girl suggests that you head to a lesbian bar for a nightcap . . . something shudders, your palms feel funny, and you find yourself revising.

I should probably point out here, before I go any farther, that Stephanie was crazy. I mean this in the purest, most straightforward sense of the word. As in she talked to herself. As in when she went to bars she stole the wineglasses, and once outside she'd throw them against a wall, any wall, or toss them up into the sky and watch them shatter on the pavement, laughing manically as she ran away. She was almost always angry at me, or angry at something else, but I was the thing in front of her, next to her, under her, so often it seemed like me, became me. Her entire back was a tattoo that made no sense. Something involving wings, a lightning bolt, a harp. At night we would drink and she'd say something along the lines of, "Let's break into the Leroy Street pool and go swimming," and we'd do it. I was new to New York then, and this was a time when everyone I was getting to know was self-aware to the point of self-paralysis, no exchange or conversation complete until it referenced, winkingly, the fact that it was an Exchange or Conversation. Stephanie, though, was something else entirely. Stephanie was unhinged, uninhibited. Stephanie was all instinct. Also, Stephanie was an alcoholic with an impressive coke habit, which is probably all I had to say in the first place.

My point is that when this unhinged and uninhibited woman suggested Henrietta's I had no reason not to take the next few obvious steps in my head. The threesome, for starters. Me in the middle, dizzy and sated, some strange woman's smooth calves clamped around my neck. The part where I am forced to sit in a chair in a corner and watch as Stephanie and a bisexual who looks remarkably like Christy Turlington show me just how worthless I am—before concluding that, actually, I'm not worthless at all, but needed, and needed badly, at which point I am untied from the chair and invited to join them. "Let's go to Henrietta Hudson's," she said, but of course what she meant was: let this be your many-hours-long indoctrination into the world of dating a bisexual woman, for real, no more coy rooftop discussions. I'd stayed up late as a boy watching *Red Shoe Diaries* on Showtime and a million *Wild Orchid* spin-offs on Cinemax. I had seen the infomercials for *Girls Gone*

Wild. If there was one thing I knew about, it was how lesbians behaved in the presence of men. I knew that, really, their interest in girls was really all about their interest in us.

Well.

As we walked inside Stephanie peeled my hand from her waist, which didn't quite fit into my idea of how things should feel.

"Hey—"

"I'll be right back," she said.

"But—"

But she was already gone. Disappeared, vanished, pulled away. At first I remained giddy and optimistic, and assumed she was simply searching for the most dainty, antibutch, non-lesbian-seeming lesbian to bring home with us. But when two minutes turned to twenty, and twenty turned to forty, I started to have doubts. I stood still, stared at my feet. I wasn't uncomfortable so much as unnoticed and, therefore, being a man, bored. The women all seemed to look through me, as if I were someone's little cousin, visiting for the weekend from a land they had no interest in hearing about. I tried to flirt harmlessly with a woman who assumed I was gay, and merely laughed when I tried to explain this wasn't the case, that I was here with my girlfriend, who I was having trouble finding. I ordered a beer and went to the pool table. I put four quarters down, figuring these girls had no chance against a man, and found myself out forty bucks soon after. When I finally located Stephanie, an hour later, someone else's finger was in her mouth.

"Hey there," I said.

"Oh, hey," Stephanie said absently.

"I see what you mean," said the woman, cryptically, as she looked at me.

It was not jealousy I felt, not in the least. It was exclusion. Invisibility. Irrelevance. What did she mean? What had Stephanie said? What the hell was this? To make matters worse, when we got home that night Stephanie passed out in the elevator and, annoyed, I carried her into my apartment and put her to bed on the coffee table. I figured in the morning she'd forget the whole thing, and, should she need a female fix in the future, she would not bring me along, which is all I really wanted.

I was wrong. In the weeks following that night there was a shift in what I'm reluctant to call "our relationship," given that what I'm describing here barely lasted two months. Anyway, apparently that evening was something of a test, and I'd been okayed, initiated into Phase Two of something I had no interest in. Suddenly I found myself regularly feeling invisible—at Henrietta's, at Ruby Fruit's, at Meow Mix. I barbequed at lesbian barbeques. I cheered at a lesbian bike race. Instead of holing up with Stephanie on Sunday mornings, I became a regular at lesbian softball games, the guy who'd pick up an extra six-pack, which wasn't quite as sexy.

As it turned out, Stephanie was into men, and into women, but not into men and women. There were no threesomes. There were no orgies, and had the offer come, I would have declined it. Stephanie, so little and lithe, always found the least conventionally feminine women the most irresistible. This was not how it was supposed to be.

Maybe there is some reality to the idea that dating a bisexual person means living a kind of raw, sexually amorphous existence—or, at the very least, getting to sit on the corner of the bed from time to time while your girlfriend kisses a girl who you secretly want to be kissing. Maybe you've been there, maybe your friend has told you stories. Call me, tell me I have it all wrong. Or maybe it's that Stephanie was heroically passive-aggressive, and started treating me like a lesbian because she wanted to end things without having to end them (though, given that her brand of craziness came with a propensity for a blunt sort of anger I haven't seen since, I doubt this).

All I know is that Stephanie and I eventually broke up, during a polite conversation that involved the throwing of a wineglass against a section of wall only a few feet from my face. We no longer talked when we ran into each other on the block. I found myself suddenly interested, at least for a bit, in the least bisexual women imaginable: a Midwestern law student, a Republican from Alabama.

Eventually I moved. Last I saw Stephanie, she told me she was moving in with someone, a man, in Tribeca. She had quit drinking, or was trying to quit, thinking about it, something like that. I smiled and said, "Good for you," and I meant it. I wish them luck. I wish him luck.

Ondine Galsworth

THE SUMMER OF MY SEXUALLY AMBIGUOUS BOYFRIEND

I'm thinking my first boyfriend might have been gay. Not because he wouldn't have sex with me—well, yeah, ultimately that did add to my suspicions—but because of everything else. The Dolfin shorts, the gay bars, the perfect body, the limp penis, just to name a few indicators.

But in my defense, before you decide I'm a total idiot, I had a good excuse for my denseness: I was fourteen. Fourteen and had never been kissed. Fourteen and more than a little stunned at having such a fierce boyfriend.

The relationship started a bit like gay porn, except my character would be played by a young nubile man-child with just a little peach fuzz on his chin and hairless abs. Instead, I played me, a budding teenager who still wore braces and had finally got her unibrow under control. My scrawny body was just beginning to hint ever so slightly of something other than a bony ass, though the serious T&A wouldn't kick in until I turned sixteen.

So there I was, threading pipe. My father was a plumber, and I was his assistant for the summer. We were working in a spacious loft in the plant district. The owner, a Broadway actor, was demanding and fussy about his fancy marble fixtures, including the bidet. I first met his son, Byron, as I was bent over a workbench (commence bad porn Muzak now). I was in overalls, pink patent leather construction boots, hair down to my butt, probably in braids, and as I said, I was threading pipe, back in the day when you had to do it by hand with a pipe threader. I was perspiring. Suddenly, through a beam of light on the floor that shimmered through the factory windows, a pair of long, golden barefooted legs sauntered by. I froze. Did a naked man just walk by? Should I look? My imagination immediately started cranking out possibilities. Another Broadway star? Someone from *Oh! Calcutta!* Maybe Raul Julia? A scraping sound high above my head startled me. I turned my whole body in slow-motion (cue theme from *2001: A Space Odyssey*), and saw Byron up on a ladder, strapping, naked, except for a pair of tiny red Dolfin shorts with white piping, his long Atlas arms stretched high above him scraping paint off the windows, his back muscles rippling, his hair lighter than blond, almost white, parted in the middle, feathering back, David Cassidy shag, skin like tupelo honey. Holy crap.

I'm from Queens. They don't even have blonds in Queens. I had yet to speak to a boy, I was a virgin, never played spin the bottle, I was a dork, and here was this Adonis.

He was nineteen, almost twenty. He smiled at me.

We went to Unity Church on our first date. What a nice guy. He wore a blue-and-white seersucker suit that showed the outline of his G.I. Joe–shaped back when he walked into the sunlight: perfect V. He smelled of Aramis. I was a wreck.

I was in junior high, barely had boobs, I thought I had a crush on a green-eyed Puerto Rican ninth-grader, but now I had this man-creature. Would I get to touch the man-body? Which part? I wanted to squeeze him like a Nerf ball.

Our relationship flourished. We went to movies, good restaurants, he had rich friends who lived in the UN Plaza. He proudly showed me off to his friends. He seemed to adore me. He called me every night. He critiqued my ensembles.

Maroon T-shirts: yes.

Barrettes: no.

Jeans with pink wedges: yes.

Jean skirts: no.

Dingo boots: yes.

We kissed on our third date just as we got off the 7 train. I wasn't prepared, I was chewing gum, I shoved it behind my back molar. He stood in a wide stance to shorten himself and bent his head toward me and stuck his tongue in my mouth. How did I get so lucky?

We were all blown away. My little Colombian mother and even littler Colombian grandmother both stood with their mouths open as I brought my six-foot-two blue-eyed gringo through the door.

He took me on a date to the city every Saturday night. We fooled around in the loft for hours. We made out naked, fondled—he liked my nipples. His body was rock hard, except for his penis. I played with it, pet it like you would a cockatoo, stroking the head gingerly, running my fingertips down its silky body. He kind of liked it. The fact that he never ejaculated didn't faze me. I was happy with our emphasis on second base, happy to touch his chest, his triceps, his blond pubic hair. We went to great bars. Some straight, above Fourteenth Street. Some gay, below Fourteenth on Seventh Avenue. The trips to the straight bars included his friend Manny, who I think had fucked every nurse from St. Vincent's. Often, I'd be left with these nurses as they lit their Virginia Slims and talked about how many abortions they'd had. We all nodded to each other knowingly, they with their big hoop earrings gleaming inside their big hair, me with my BonneBell lip gloss and my hymen firmly in place.

I especially loved the gay bars. This was back when leather boys and fems were more pronounced, before gay became assimilated into the mainstream (you know what I mean, let's not get political, I was fourteen, okay? I loved the outfits). I would sit and watch the mating dance (cue Donna Summer, since it was actually playing). Big guys with bulging muscles and giant bulges were playing pool two feet in front of me. They were scary and exciting, tough guys with tattoos, Marlboros tucked under their shirtsleeves, worn-out jeans, no underwear. They looked at me fondly, as if I were a cute Pomeranian, or more likely, a very young girl in Gloria Vanderbilts, sitting very still, sipping her illegal vodka-and-cran. To me, they were just men squared, mega-men who wore their testosterone on the outside. They were sexual, but totally safe for me, kind of like a peep show for my burgeoning sexuality. I was so fascinated by these men that I forgot to ask myself why it was that we, Byron and I, were here exactly. Why did he know some of the guys by name? Why was he so impressed with the really good pool player with the dog collar? Why did he whisper in my ear, "The big one with the vest, that's his bitch over there"? Really? I asked. That little guy with the Tony Orlando mustache?

Why did Byron cover all of his shoes with a hand-kerchief? The dust, he would say. Why did his face-washing routine involve five products? Clinique, I think. I liked that he was tidy. I was a slob, had never made a bed, my room was a horror show, his was relaxing, everything in its place. I loved the way he folded his clothes.

Then, after a really fun year, he gave me perfume, I gave him a bracelet inscribed I LOVE YOU, and then he said it was time we had sex. Sex? Intercourse. Shit man, no way, I was still just fourteen. So we broke up and he joined the navy. I know, shut up. Cue Village People.

A few years later, freshly deflowered, I was determined to find Byron and show him my new skills. Luckily he found me. He called, said we should hang out. We made out in a car, it was weird, he took off my clothes, licked my inner thigh, then invited me to a party at the loft. There were people doing

drugs all over the place—whippets, poppers, coke. I had a beer
and dragged Byron to a dark corner to work my magic.

For hours, we tried. Like, three hours. The kissing was
great, the fondling not bad, the semi flopping around inside me—
not so good. We kept trying. He grabbed my boobs, kissed my
belly, I grabbed his schlong, put it in my mouth, got a response,
did a 180 and jumped on, felt it deflate inside me, jumped off,
put it in my mouth, sprung back on, jumped off, did the two-
hands-twisting-back-and-forth-on-the-shaft thing as I made
circles with my tongue, hopped back on, tried all my new fancy
moves, up and down, grinding, straddle. Nothing. We talked.
He seemed cranky, distracted, annoyed. More kissing. Finally
he handed me off to his giant, gross hairy friend Pedro. Six-
foot-five, beard, back fur, naked, and breathing all over me,
"Come on, I'm here, you're here, it's perfect." I wasn't listening.
I was wondering why Byron didn't want me. Was it the coke?
I was hurt, and yes, clueless, naive, young. I kept Pedro at bay
until the sun rose and then dragged my crestfallen self home.

I always saw my disastrous night with Byron as a black
mark on my lipstick case. It wasn't until one night while driving across the country with a girlfriend, somewhere in the
Midwest in a Motel 6, after hours of discussing men, including details of my first great love Byron, that I had my great
epiphany: "Oh my God, Byron was gay!"

"Well, duh!" she said as she rolled over to go to sleep.
"But he sounds like a great boyfriend."

Henry Sutton

TREADING WATER IN THE MEDITERRANEAN

Frankly, the sex was pretty second-rate. I certainly fancied her enough, but there was always a reticence on her part. She didn't want to do it as often as I did, and she wasn't very keen on exploring the more athletic aspects of foreplay, oral sex, or intercourse. As for anal sex, I don't think she'd ever heard of the term, let alone contemplated the reality. She didn't like it when I took her from behind. She didn't like it when I kissed her too vigorously.

However, as I implied, she kept me keen. Actually, it was one of those terrible relationships when you have to masturbate all the time because you are constantly aroused but not getting anything like enough action. Indeed, one night, long after I'd turned over, frustrated, and should have been fast asleep, I heard a rustling and sensed rapid movement under the duvet.

She was masturbating. I couldn't believe it. Apart from the fact that I found this incredibly erotic and instantly wanted to join in, I couldn't understand why she was doing it.

"What are you doing?" I said stupidly.

"What do you think?" she replied, quite breathless.

"Why?" I said, moving closer.

"Because it helps me sleep," she said.

"I could have done it for you," I said. "Or we could have done something else. Together."

I can't exactly remember what she said to that, but it was along the lines of her not feeling like it, and that her masturbating was not really a sexual thing, but simply a mechanism to help her nod off. I think she might even have used the phrase "my little helper." What could I do? There was another reason behind her furtive masturbating, but I didn't find that out until years later. Long after we'd broken up.

In the meantime, we trundled along for quite a bit longer, fighting on and off. In fact we fought quite a lot. She slapped me once, hard, on the steps of an exclusive London drinking club. I think I had refused to rise to the bait over something she was getting steamed up about and for once had ignored her. She didn't like to be ignored when she was cross.

Amazingly, that summer we even went on holiday, to France. In reality it was a sort of make-or-break trip. However, something really quite extraordinary happened there. It was of little consequence to the future of our relationship, but it was an incident that I'll certainly never forget, and in many ways was quite a defining moment. At least it makes me think about who I am and where I came from, and why sex is so loaded with the past, and can be so explosive in the present, and just how very salty the Mediterranean was.

A friend of her parents lent us their villa in the Camargue. Ever been to the Camargue? It's heaven and hell. For a great, flat watery chunk of the south of France, it's remarkably undeveloped. The place is still inhabited by wild ponies and Gypsies. Flamingos fly by every evening. It should be a place of high romance, catching up with sunsets and hooking into a wild, unspoiled way of life. Except for the mosquitoes. It's virtually impossible to sit outside after about five in the evening. The mosquitoes are fucking killers. No wonder the Camargue is so unspoiled. No wonder hardly anyone ever goes there.

Needless to say, the holiday got off to an appalling start. As if I didn't already know, my girlfriend was something of a neurotic. She became obsessed with plastering herself with every known brand of mosquito repellent, whatever the time of day. She smelled, and tasted, disgusting. Which, of course, was a huge shame, because the villa was very secluded and came with a pool, and it would have been a perfect place to wander around naked. But what was I thinking? I knew my girlfriend had issues with her body, or rather her sense of her body. She never would have wandered around naked, despite the mosquitoes, or the strong Mediterranean sun—she was equally obsessed with not getting sunburned as not getting bitten.

So, to her various layers of mosquito repellent she applied thick layers of sunscreen, only adding to the horrible smell and taste of her, but not completely disguising her looks. She was still gorgeous, with big dark eyes and long luscious brown wavy hair, pert breasts and a shapely arse, and long slender legs. I still desired her hugely. But she was not going anywhere near me, and it wasn't too pleasant going too near her. We watched the flamingos from behind the mosquito netting, then argued about what we were going to eat for dinner. She had very complicated issues with food, too, which she was loath to discuss in detail, but would allude to constantly. By the time we'd settled on some utterly benign dish, I'd have drunk too much local rosé—about the only good thing to drink in the Camargue—and she would decide that actually she wasn't hungry anyway.

We would go to bed fractious and starved, and immediately lie as far apart as possible on the sticky, lumpy mattress in the sweltering room. There was no air-conditioning, and her paranoia about being invaded by an army of mosquitoes meant that we couldn't simply close the shutters and nets, we had to have the windows firmly sealed as well.

One day, we actually got as far as the beach in Saintes-Maries-de-la-Mer. Maybe she was at last feeling sorry for me. Maybe I was feeling sorry for her. Either way, we hit the beach in a bright, playful mood. It was just like old times, not that I could really remember what those times were, or whether we'd even had any.

She had perhaps gone a little lighter on the mosquito repellent and the sunscreen, because she wasn't smelling too awful, and I might have leaned over and kissed her as we stepped onto the sand. She stripped to her swimming costume—she was not the sort of girl who wore a bikini, even though she more than had the figure for it—and laid out her towel and settled down with her book and her cigarettes. All I could do was admire her glistening body, packed tight and curvy in that navy costume. Then I had an idea.

"How about renting a pedalo?" I said.

"Yeah, okay," she said, sitting up.

"Really?" I said.

"Sure," she said. "It might be fun."

That was a word I hadn't heard for a while.

For such an out-of-the-way beach, it was sort of strange that there was a pedalo operation, not that it was doing great business. We were the first people to take one out that day. It was of the old style. More wood than plastic, with rusty, stiff pedals and a rudder that was almost impossible to turn. Once aboard, we set a course for the horizon and kept pedaling.

The Mediterranean was mill-pond flat, and out on the still water the heat seemed to be even more intense, turning the blue sky white. It was like we were floating into a haze. We were both sweating profusely, and after I don't know how much longer, she said, "I'm going for a swim," then jumped off the side. I joined her, and in the water we did something we hadn't done all holiday. We embraced. Treading water, I ran my hands over her lovely bottom and unbelievably, she felt for my cock.

Back on board, I said, "Why don't we?" I could barely see the shore, and there were no other boats or pedalos in anything like the vicinity. "How?" she said, which I took to be a very encouraging sign. "I don't know," I said. There was nowhere to lie down and the double cockpit was really just two hard, slatted, wooden seats, with huge pedals in the way. "You could sit on me."

Which was exactly what she did. She stood up, awkwardly, pulled her costume off, and clambered over to my side of the boat and sat on me, face first. We started kissing, properly, and I could tell she was getting aroused by the way she was grinding herself into my lap. Almost instantly I had an erection, but it took another awkward maneuver for me to remove my trunks and enter her. She was totally wet and slippery, and tasted of salt, and I didn't think I could hold on for her to come. I was bursting, and had long forgotten who might be watching. But she always came quickly and easily, perhaps too quickly, and this time, out on the water, it was no different.

I remember watching a dollop of come drip out of her as she climbed off me, and returned to her side of the cockpit. We split up shortly after that holiday. The next time I saw her, some two years later, she was living with a woman. I often wonder whether she's told her girlfriend about the time she had sex at sea. I doubt it somehow. But I never told her that I'd lost my virginity on a boat. It wasn't at sea but on a river. I was ridiculously young. So was my then-girlfriend. And it wasn't anything like as much fun or as passionate as out on that pedalo.

Jonathan Goldstein
MARATHON MAN

For some reason, when I was eighteen, on the rare occasion I was able to convince a woman to sleep with me, afterward, as we lay in bed naked, I would become terribly depressed.

I still can't say what exactly it was, and as I got older the feeling left me alone. But at that time, I was very sensitive and had to tread lightly in the arena of sex. Blowjobs left me feeling lonely and vulnerable. Sixty-nines made me feel claustrophobic, like I was being buried alive. Even massages made me anxious, more conscious of my own blood-and-gutness than was to my taste.

The only sex act I found myself comfortable with was the handjob. There was something about it that felt easy and conversational. It was like going for coffee with a friend, but with your dick included in the chat. And I should say that even in the h.j. department, I wasn't exactly laid back. So used to the way I handjobbed myself, it took me a good ten minutes just to acclimatize to another person's touch. Once we got going, I needed a lot of encouragement—reassuring talk, oils, balms, and constant repositioning. Plus, a decade of self-abuse had rendered my dick pretty much aristocratically indifferent. I had to practically slam it in a doorjamb to get it halfway turgid. So a typical handjob usually took anywhere between twenty to thirty minutes, with me shouting "harder!" and "faster!" like I was whipping a team of snow dogs across the tundra.

Of all the fist fellatio I received during that unfortunate period, the most grueling, soul-debilitating, and dehumanizing took place in my parents' basement. It was midnight. I was hanging out with my girlfriend, Amy, drinking beer and listening to the local classic rock station when she told me to lean back on the couch and take off my pants.

Tired, slightly drunk, and not especially aroused, I still did as I was told, and as I did so, she took off upstairs to look for paraphernalia.

"There's some ointment in the downstairs bathroom," I said.

"I never want to hear you use that word," she said. "It turns me off."

Amy was the kind of overachiever who prided herself on getting the job done, the type who made bird feeders, baked complicated pastries, and taught herself to play the French horn. I was the kind of guy who used words like "ointment."

I'll never forget how hopeful and sweet she looked trotting down the stairs, her arms loaded with pharmaceuticals, so completely unaware of the handjobathon we were about to embark on. It was like the beginning of that Stephen King novel *The Long Walk*, where all the kids show up, well rested and fresh-faced, about to embark on the never-ending jaunt that would eventually kill them.

The start was pretty promising. Despite the three or four beers in me, I became erect easily. She pounded away, looking at me, looking at the ceiling, smiling, sighing. After fifteen minutes, she stopped to massage her wrist.

"You don't have to continue," I said.

"No, I want to," she said.

I guess she was still under the impression that leaving a job unfinished could prove a blemish on her sexual résumé. So she carried on, as though getting me off were some kind of logic problem that could be solved through perseverance. She brought to it all of the overachieving eagerness she brought to all of her undertakings. It was like doing a thorough job on a bibliography or getting out a grape-juice stain. Nothing a little old-fashioned elbow grease and determination couldn't resolve.

She started up again, her fist pogoing up and down, her fingers doing fancy little French-horny things. I watched, unimpressed. Twenty minutes in, my mind began to wander: *Was this what that song from* Grease, *"Hand Jive," was really about? Is that what we were doing? Hand jive? Can there really exist an orgasm machine like the one from* Young Frankenstein? *Have my friends just been giving me a good time or am I really that great a dungeon master?*

Amy let go and rolled her hand around on her wrist, her mouth wide open in mock/real pain.

"Are you even enjoying this?" she asked.

"Of course," I lied.

What exactly is headcheese? Who's next in line for president after the speaker of the house?

After another spirited half-hour, she introduced her left hand to the equation, using it to manhandle my balls. It was like watching one of those science films of a Neanderthal trying to start a fire. Yet somehow I remained, all throughout, as hard as a ketchup bottle.

Two A.M. came and went. I started drifting in and out of consciousness. I'd have these quick two-second dreams where I'm riding a unicycle along a bumpy gravel road. I'd reawaken with a start to find her pounding away, no longer even looking at me, dropping the charade of eye contact and focused solely on my penis. It was as if she were enacting an age-old primordial tale. Like a sexualized version of *The Old Man and the Sea*, this had become a test of endurance between her and my dick.

"You are a worthy opponent, but come you shall."

The clock on the VCR read three A.M. Aside from a few cigarette breaks and a couple chats about "what the hell was the matter here," they had been at it, my penis and her, for three hours straight. I felt completely alienated from her, from my own penis. From life itself.

I decided to take a shortcut to the finish line. I closed my eyes and imagined myself in my eleventh-grade classroom being masturbated by Mrs. Velardi, our thirty-something art teacher who wore tank tops and bandanas. Then, in the midst of it all, in walked Amy. I saw her, wearing the same thing she was wearing beside me on the couch, but instead of being flesh and blood, she was imaginary—entirely in my head.

Oddly, closing my eyes and imagining being jacked off by Amy was more titillating than keeping my eyes open and watching the actual thing. It made it more perverted somehow, and thus transported me to the next level.

"Faster," I whispered. "Harder."

The radio was blasting a Doobie Brothers retrospective. I reached over and turned it off in the middle of "Taking It to the Streets." The Doobie Brotherless silence was all I needed, and thirty seconds later I was an out-of-control garden hose.

I remember Amy raising her hands in the air, triumphant, like that freeze-frame of Judd Nelson at the end of *The Breakfast Club*.

The next day, I had to wrap my penis in toilet paper to keep it from rubbing against my jeans. It was bruised and battered, but also oddly naked—lonely without a hand wrapped around it, pole-dancing to classic rock 'n' roll. Eventually, of course, it would grow most comfortable in its aloneness, but just then it needed coddling.

Sarah Hepola
MANUAL LABOR

At one A.M. on a Friday night, I stood in the personal care aisle of Wal-Mart.

Obviously, I was drunk.

Beside me, my friend Bob rummaged through a shelf of personal massagers—undulating nylon mats and giant, thumping devices that could clock someone—in search of an item he'd dubbed "the Cadillac of vibrators."

"They're out," said Bob, his body half-buried in scattered boxes. "But this might work."

"This?" I turned the white box over in my hand. "It looks like a hand-mixer."

He sighed. "This is more like the Grand Am of vibrators. The Ford Escort of vibrators."

"How does it even work?" I asked.

Bob gave me a look. He'd taken me this far. From here, I was on my own.

Earlier that night, Bob and I had been in a smoky dive, drinking pitchers of lager and admitting things we shouldn't have. Like the number of people we'd slept with, and when, and how, and why. We weren't lovers; we were beer buddies who reveled in this kind of conversational striptease. Inevitably, though, it went a smidge too far, like the time Bob told me his testicles were unusually large. Or the time, that night, when I made the more-than-slightly-embarrassing revelation that I'd never had an orgasm.

Bob was incredulous. "Never, ever?"

I shook my head and lit a cigarette.

"Don't you have a vibrator?"

"Keep it down!" I said, squirming in my seat.

"Why are you freaking out?" asked Bob. "There's nothing wrong with having a vibrator."

"Stop saying that so loud," I whispered.

"What, vibrator? What's wrong with you?" asked Bob.

I wasn't sure. But I was beginning to suspect that—despite a lifetime of pretending otherwise—I was a bit of a prude.

How did it happen? In kindergarten, I was the kid who told unbelieving listeners on the playground where babies come from. In sixth grade, I passed around *The Color Purple* in French class. It was dog-eared to the page where one woman tells another to hold a mirror up to her "you-know-what" and admire it. In high school, I had sex earlier and more often than my girlfriends, who came to me for advice: like what lingerie to wear, how to lie across the bed so your thighs look thinner, which angle was most flattering.

And therein lay the problem. By age seventeen, I had swallowed so many movie fantasies about what sex was supposed to look like—torso arched in ecstasy, toes curled comically—that I didn't bother to ask how it was supposed to feel. And it felt . . . okay. But there was no white-hot ecstasy, no explosion of bliss. My boyfriend was incredibly attentive, valiant when it came to my pleasure, and so, not wanting to disappoint him, I did exactly what they do in the movies.

I faked it.

By the time I got to college, girls had changed. They were no longer shy about sex; they talked openly about their orgasm, about masturbating, about always being on top. They made me uneasy, like fluent speakers in a language I was still stumbling through. I had a friend, a gorgeous woman who slung around her sexuality like a bright-blue feather boa, and one night, I admitted my own little problem.

"Oh, honey, lots of women can't come during sex," she told me, holding up two fingers like bunny ears. "That's why you have to treat yourself."

She gave me a book from her shelf. Inside was a sketch of a woman with her legs spread, her labia diagrammed like a topographical map. That night, and several nights after, I took a warm bath and got into bed early. I turned the light off and pulled my pajamas around my ankles.

And I felt so stupid.

Stupid, like someone was watching me and cracking jokes. After all, this was the scene in the movie where someone walks in, someone catches you in the breathless sneer of pleasure and you're left to clamber for composure, utterly exposed. Eventually, I turned the light back on, defeated, and read myself to sleep.

And that's how I got to be twenty-five without having an orgasm.

"I know a really good vibrator," Bob continued. (Bob, I suspect, had the polar opposite relationship with masturbation.) "It's the Cadillac of vibrators."

No way. No way was I slinking into some neon-lit smut shop at midnight with Bob, slapping down sixty-five dollars for a hot pink windup cock, or a "rabbit," or whatever desperate single girls bought these days.

"They sell it at Wal-Mart," he said.

Wal-Mart? The store that only sells edited versions of rap songs?

"It's a personal massager," Bob explained.

"I already have a massager," I said. "It's for your back." Every year for Christmas, my mom gave me some widget for relieving back pain, stressed feet, or cold hands.

Bob looked at me as if I'd just sent a letter to Santa Claus.

"Really?" I whispered.

"The Cad-il-lac of vibrators," Bob said, savoring each syllable.

Bob dropped me off at home that night with the zeal of a parent leaving his daughter at prom. "Have fun!" he waved enthusiastically. "Tell me how it goes!"

I went inside. I made a drink. I watched a little late-night television, flipped through a glossy magazine. Eventually I could not avoid it any longer: I had to use that thing.

I have told this story many times. Always during one of those wonderfully cozy, drunk confessional exchanges, like the conversation with Bob that started the whole thing in the first place. The you-show-me-yours-I'll-show-you-mine of our adulthood. The story works because it is honest, and a little painful, and because for so many of us, first times are less steamy romance, more comedy caper. It's not that I wanted to feel sexy, exactly. I was alone. I was unwatched. I held a machine that made the approximate noise of an electric shaver. But damn those movies. Damn those women and their perfect silhouettes. No matter what sexual adventure I attempted, a thousand soft-focus films had made it tough—even in the privacy of my bedroom, in the hush and hum of three A.M.—to overcome the sense, the creeping and hideous suggestion, that I was doing it wrong.

Trust me, I was. I sat at the edge of my bed, because the cord wouldn't reach all the way. When I touched the plastic knob to my flesh, the electric surge was so strong that it sent me clattering to the floor, cross-eyed and frightened.

I was humiliated. Was everyone this inept, or was it just me? Was the orgasm just another one of those golden gifts—like long, shapely legs or straight hair or discretion—bestowed on people at birth, but that somehow passed me by?

I lay in bed that night, feeling sorry for myself. I would never return to Wal-Mart. I would never buy the Cadillac of vibrators. In fact, it took two weeks to get the nerve to call Bob again, and almost a year to tell him the whole story. I did, however, remember one thing. On my bedside table—right under my nose, almost literally—sat a tiny, pocket-sized back massager, a gift from my mother that sat beside my table lamp and alarm clock, collecting dust. I reached over in the dark to see if the battery still worked.

It did.

Claudia Lonow
THE REAL ME

They say no one can love you till you love yourself. But if you don't love yourself in the first place, it's probably also true that you don't respect your own opinion, so even if you did start loving yourself, would you care?

Yet paradoxically, people want other people to love them for who they really are, deep down inside, even though they themselves don't. Which would be fine, except that when they do unearth this so-called real self and tell you their deep, true, inner feelings, they're never good feelings. They never say, "Hey! I'm secretly really happy!" It's always more like, "Hey, you know that funny guy who dresses well, paid for dinner, and is in love with you? That's not the real me. The real me is an overly critical ambivalent asshole. Now, how's about a hug?"

And I'm like, let's get back to the lying. This isn't my real hair color. These aren't even my real eyelashes. You think this is my real personality? Of course not. No one has seen the real me since I was eight years old and got kicked out of my tent in sleep-away camp. And good thing, too. The real me is a needy, chubby, coked up, drunken whore who likes to lie in bed all day masturbating to the gang-rape scenes in *A Clockwork Orange*.

When my ex-boyfriend began revealing his true self, everything started going downhill. I met him at an anonymous HIV testing center (negative again, yay!). I guess I really shouldn't say that, so if you run into him don't tell him about this piece. Of course, to run into him you'd have to be in his apartment, since he never leaves it. However, if you want to hide from him while *in* his apartment, go in the shower, since he doesn't take any. He has sadly interpreted the whole "I'm going to be my real self" concept to mean "my real self without soap and water."

When we first met, though, he washed and everything was fine. He had no job and four ex-wives—kind of a red flag. But he did have things going for him, like: he was once a photographer for *Der Spiegel*, used to lived with a porn star, and claimed he could come five times in one night if he'd gotten enough sleep the night before. Also, he looked like Peter O'Toole, and I like sleeping with people who look like famous people.

As time went on, though, I noticed him doing and saying things that were unnerving. Some of them weren't surprises, they were just things I'd initially overlooked. Like the fact that he sometimes spoke with a German accent because he'd spent some time there. Other annoying traits included criticizing everything I did, saying the phrase "great minds think alike" with the implication that his was one of the great minds, and asking me to fuck him in the ass with a strap-on, which is easier said than done, and actually, not even that easy to say.

But I'm a people pleaser, so we go to the Pleasure Palace, and with the help of a three-hundred-pound lesbian, make our way past the eight-foot cocks, leather masks, and amazingly lifelike foam pussy molds to the strap-on-dildo section. We pick out the least sexual and most utilitarian one, take it home, and commence a tension-filled preparatory makeout session, after which we undress and try to get the dildo out of its package, which ultimately requires the use of a box cutter.

I fumble around trying to get the strap-on strapped on, and since I'm stone-cold sober I start to wonder whether I'd been accurate in blaming alcohol for all the questionable things I'd done in the past. For instance, I'd always thought booze was the culprit behind me fucking this guy I'd just met in the pool during a party. But clearly I could no longer blame that on being drunk because I don't even need to be drunk to put on a fake penis. And the sight of my boyfriend lying there waiting for me to make things happen caused me to ask myself, "Is this really the guy for me? I can't even get him to give me a decent back rub. Why am I putting on a fake penis to fuck a guy with no money? I used to be on television."

But I'm not on television anymore. He's laying on his stomach as I sit on his tush, the rubber cock lightly bouncing off his back. I touch my new penis for a minute to see if having this extra appendage will make me feel more powerful, more entitled, more prone to declarative statements like, "Get me my dinner, bitch," and, "You're fired." No. No, it doesn't. It just feels like a weird dead thing hanging off me, a phantom limb.

I turn on the bedroom lamp so I can see what I'm doing. This is a major mistake. It turns out my boyfriend's asshole isn't his best feature. Maybe it looks like Peter O'Toole's asshole, but who's to say? It's darker than the skin around it and, upon closer inspection, proves to be hairier than one might expect. I'd be losing my erection now if it weren't constructed of high-density silicone. But how does one back out of a thing like this? I made a promise. A promise to violate him, and I don't want to be the girl who promised to violate someone and then, in the crucial moments leading up to the experience, backs out. That would make me an Indian giver.

I put a little lubricant on my finger and apply it appropriately. Immediately, he starts moaning. This makes me feel good about myself. Already I'm a hit. Maybe this won't be so bad. Maybe this is my calling. I lift myself up with one arm, grab my faux dick with the other, and try to insert it, which will bring my man to heights of pleasure heretofore unknown.

Well, I can't get it in. What some of you probably don't know about strap-ons is that because the dick isn't fastened to anything stable, like a torso, it slips all around and you have to hold on to it as you're trying to maneuver it. This requires skill and grace, qualities I lack even while walking across a room, let alone trying to wedge a slippery object into a tense, expectant sphincter.

I don't know why, but it doesn't help that he keeps critiquing me in the German accent and barking orders like, "Just squirt the tube of KY directly into my asshole." I think to myself, "You know what? It's not that simple, okay? I'm the one doing all the work, and I would appreciate a little gratitude. I mean, who's the bottom here, honey? Let's try being a little more submissive."

But I don't say any of that and finally, we give up. Not only does the whole thing turn out to be a disaster, but with all the KY around, neither of us can unbuckle the strap-on and I have to walk around wearing it until our hands crust over.

No pun intended, but hindsight being 20/20, it's now clear to me why it was so hard. I've subsequently learned from watching porn that fucking someone in the ass ain't easy. You have to know what you're doing. And, in actuality, what with being a woman and all, I didn't really even know how to fuck a vagina. I'd had mine fucked, of course, but I hadn't ever really paid attention to how that was being accomplished.

I can see now that my ex wasn't the person I thought he was when we met. And neither was I. He was secretly weaker and I was secretly stronger. And I still don't know if the real me is the girl who stayed with him all those years, never telling him how I really felt about anything, or the girl who finally just walked away, dragging her dick behind her.

ABOUT THE AUTHORS

Steve Almond is the author of the nonfiction book *Candyfreak* and the story collections *My Life in Heavy Metal* and *The Evil B.B. Chow and Other Stories*. His latest collection will be published this year.

Jonathan Ames is the author of *I Pass Like Night; The Extra Man; What's Not to Love?; My Less Than Secret Life;* and *Wake Up, Sir!* He is the winner of a Guggenheim Fellowship and is a former columnist for *New York Press*. His latest book is *I Love You More Than You Know*.

David Amsden is a contributor to *New York* magazine and the author of a novel, *Important Things That Don't Matter*.

Jami Attenberg has written about sex, technology, design, graphic novels, and urban life for Salon.com, *Print, Nylon,* and the *San Francisco Chronicle*. She is the author of a story collection, *Instant Love,* and a novel, *The Kept Man*.

Shalom Auslander is the author of *Foreskin's Lament*, a memoir, and *Beware of God*, which was a finalist for the 2005 Koret Award for Writers Under 35. His writing has appeared in the *New Yorker*, *Esquire*, and the *New York Times Magazine*, and he is a regular contributor to Public Radio International's *This American Life*.

Arthur Bradford's first book, *Dogwalker*, was published by Knopf in 2001, and as a Vintage paperback in 2002. He is also the director of *How's Your News?*, a series of documentary films featuring news reporters with mental disabilities, which has appeared on HBO/Cinemax, PBS, and Trio.

Ben Brown is an Internet rockstar. He lives in San Francisco, but dreams of Austin, Texas.

Lisa Carver lives in New Hampshire. She started the 'zine *Roller-derby* and for several years wrote the column "The Lisa Diaries" for Nerve.com. She is the author of the books *Dancing Queen* and *Drugs Are Nice*, and she has written for *Newsday*, *Playboy*, *Utne Reader*, *Details*, and *Glamour*.

Ari Cohen's writing has appeared in the *New York Times* and *Marie Claire*. She lives in Manhattan.

Will Doig has written for *New York* magazine, *Out*, *BlackBook*, and *Highlights for Children*. He was raised in Massachusetts and New Hampshire. Today he lives in Park Slope, Brooklyn.

Monica Drake's fiction has appeared in the *Beloit Fiction Review,* the *Threepenny Review,* the *Insomniac Reader,* and other magazines. She teaches at the Pacific Northwest College of Art in Portland, Oregon. *Clown Girl* is her first novel.

Lisa Gabriele's writing has appeared in the *Washington Post, Vice,* and the *New York Times Magazine,* and on Nerve.com and Salon .com. She directs and shoots documentaries for the Life Network, the History Channel, and the CBC. Her first novel, *Tempting Faith DiNapoli,* was published by Simon and Schuster. She lives in Toronto, where she's at work on her second book.

Ondine Galsworth is working on a novel about her experiences as a go-go dancer. A New York native, she now lives in New Jersey.

Jonathan Goldstein's writing has appeared in *ReadyMade, Land-Grant College Review,* the *Carolina Quarterly,* and the *New York Times.* His first novel, *Lenny Bruce Is Dead,* was published in America in 2006. He was born in Brooklyn and lives in Montreal.

Sarah Hepola has been a high school teacher, a playwright, a film critic, a music editor, and a travel columnist. Her work has appeared in the *New York Times,* the *Guardian,* and on NPR and Slate.com. She lives in Williamsburg, Brooklyn.

Abeer Hoque is the winner of the 2005 Tanenbaum Award for non-fiction and the 2006–7 Fulbright Scholarship. Her stories, poems, and photographs have been published in *ZYZZYVA, 580 Split, Switchback,* the *Pittsburgh Post-Gazette,* and on BullfightReview.com. She was born in Nigeria and lives in Bangladesh.

Kevin Keck will probably come and stay on your couch for an extended period of time if you ask him to. He will pay for any phone calls he makes from your house.

Porochista Khakpour's writing has appeared in the *Village Voice*, the *Chicago Reader, Gear, Flaunt, Bidoun, URB, TENbyTEN*, and *Paper*. She has completed her first novel and is at work on a second.

Jen Kirkman is a writer and comedian. She has appeared on numerous television shows, including Comedy Central's *Premium Blend*, NBC's *Late Friday*, and Oxygen's *Hey Monie!* She also performs live at the Hollywood Improv, the Laugh Factory, the M Bar and Restaurant, and the Comedy Central Workspace. She lives in Los Angeles.

Claudia Lonow played the chubby, loud-mouthed daughter of Michele Lee on *Knots Landing*, and has made appearances on *The Love Boat, Fantasy Island*, and *Beverly Hills, 90210*. She's the creator of such cult TV hits as Showtime's *Rude Awakening* and *Good Girls Don't . . .* on the Oxygen Network, and has written episodes of *The War at Home* and *Less Than Perfect*. She resides on a cul-de-sac in Los Angeles.

Pasha Malla lives in Toronto. His fiction and nonfiction have appeared in a number of magazines, journals, and anthologies, including *Hobart, Maisonneuve, McSweeney's*, and *The Journey Prize Stories* 2005.

Scott Mebus is the author of *The Big Happy* and *Booty Nomad*. He is a novelist, songwriter, playwright, comic, and music producer. Previously, he was a producer for MTV and VH1, where he worked on *The Real World*, *The Tom Green Show*, and *MTV Yoga*. He lives in New York City.

Neal Pollack is the author of *The Neal Pollack Anthology of American Literature*, *Beneath the Axis of Evil*, *Never Mind the Pollacks*, and *Alternadad*. He lives in Los Angeles.

Rachel Shukert is a playwright, performance artist, and actress who can often be seen on the hallowed stages of New York if she is not in Europe, where she wastes a lot of time. She is the cofounder of the soon-to-be legendary theater company, the Bushwick Hotel.

Henry Sutton writes books about sex, death, and food. He is the books editor at the *Daily Mirror* and the literary editor for the U.K. edition of *Esquire*. He lives in south London, but was born by the sea in Norfolk and longs to go back there one day.

Sarah Thyre is an actress and writer. Her memoir, *Dark at the Roots*, was published in 2007. She lives in Los Angeles with her two children and her husband, Andy Richter.